PREFACE

Improving energy efficiency at the end-use level is increasingly important as Climate Change commitments force policy makers to look for areas where greenhouse gas emissions reduction can be achieved rapidly. Indeed, although much improvement has been made over the past 25 years, significant potential for improving energy efficiency still exists.

Labelling and minimum efficiency standards for appliances and equipment have proven to be one of the most promising policy instruments. Used for many years in some IEA Member countries, they delivered tangible results. They are among the cheapest and least intrusive of policies. Policy makers cannot afford to neglect them.

This book examines current and past experiences of countries using labels and standards to improve energy end-use efficiency. It identifies successful policy approaches, focussing on what works best. It also provides insight into the opportunities ahead, including the widespread use of computer chips in appliances, cars and equipment. This book should be of great help not only to administrations planning to introduce labelling schemes but also to those in the process of strengthening their current programmes. Policy makers in developing countries will also find here all necessary justification for implementing labelling and standards in their economy.

Robert Priddle
Executive Director

ACKNOWLEDGEMENTS

This first study in the series *Energy Efficiency Policy Profiles* is the fruit of several years of monitoring of existing programmes and gathering information, notably through expert workshops. The project formed part of the programme of the Energy Efficiency Policy Analysis Division within the IEA's Office of Energy Efficiency, Technology and R&D. John Newman, the study's author, led the project, under the guidance of Jean-Pierre Des Rosiers, and with the help of Benoit Lebot, who both contributed much valuable expertise.

Hans Joergen Koch
Director, Energy Efficiency, Technology and R&D

INTERNATIONAL ENERGY AGENCY

ENERGY LABELS
& STANDARDS

ENERGY EFFICIENCY POLICY PROFILES

OECD

INTERNATIONAL ENERGY AGENCY

9, rue de la Fédération,
75739 Paris Cedex 15, France

The International Energy Agency (IEA) is an autonomous body which was established in November 1974 within the framework of the Organisation for Economic Co-operation and Development (OECD) to implement an international energy programme.

It carries out a comprehensive programme of energy co-operation among twenty-four* of the OECD's twenty-nine Member countries. The basic aims of the IEA are:

■ To maintain and improve systems for coping with oil supply disruptions;

■ To promote rational energy policies in a global context through co-operative relations with non-member countries, industry and international organisations;

■ To operate a permanent information system on the international oil market;

■ To improve the world's energy supply and demand structure by developing alternative energy sources and increasing the efficiency of energy use;

■ To assist in the integration of environmental and energy policies.

IEA Member countries: Australia, Austria, Belgium, Canada, Denmark, Finland, France, Germany, Greece, Hungary, Ireland, Italy, Japan, Luxembourg, the Netherlands, New Zealand, Norway, Portugal, Spain, Sweden, Switzerland, Turkey, the United Kingdom, the United States. The European Commission also takes part in the work of the IEA.

ORGANISATION FOR ECONOMIC CO-OPERATION AND DEVELOPMENT

Pursuant to Article 1 of the Convention signed in Paris on 14th December 1960, and which came into force on 30th September 1961, the Organisation for Economic Co-operation and Development (OECD) shall promote policies designed:

■ To achieve the highest sustainable economic growth and employment and a rising standard of living in Member countries, while maintaining financial stability, and thus to contribute to the development of the world economy;

■ To contribute to sound economic expansion in Member as well as non-member countries in the process of economic development; and

■ To contribute to the expansion of world trade on a multilateral, non-discriminatory basis in accordance with international obligations.

The original Member countries of the OECD are Austria, Belgium, Canada, Denmark, France, Germany, Greece, Iceland, Ireland, Italy, Luxembourg, the Netherlands, Norway, Portugal, Spain, Sweden, Switzerland, Turkey, the United Kingdom and the United States. The following countries became Members subsequently through accession at the dates indicated hereafter: Japan (28th April 1964), Finland (28th January 1969), Australia (7th June 1971), New Zealand (29th May 1973), Mexico (18th May 1994), the Czech Republic (21st December 1995), Hungary (7th May 1996), Poland (22nd November 1996) and the Republic of Korea (12th December 1996). The Commission of the European Communities takes part in the work of the OECD (Article 13 of the OECD Convention).

TABLE OF CONTENTS

4 ASSESSMENTS OF ACTUAL AND
EXPECTED RESULTS OF LABELS AND
STANDARDS IN IEA COUNTRIES 99

5 ISSUES FOR THE FUTURE 117

6 CONCLUSIONS AND
RECOMMENDATIONS 129

A APPENDIX
OVERVIEW OF CURRENT LABELS AND
STANDARDS PROGRAMMES IN IEA
COUNTRIES 139

INTRODUCTION

Home appliances and office equipment consume at least 1 100 TWh/year of electricity in IEA Member Countries, accounting for over a quarter of the region's final electricity use. This is the second fastest growing sector of energy use after private transport. In comparison these products consume considerably less electricity in Non member Countries at present, but the use is growing rapidly as living standards rise. Other household products consume 1 200 TWh of electricity and 11.3 EJ of natural gas each year.

Governments have succeeded in slowing the growth of electricity and gas use and CO_2 emissions from these residential and office products through carefully targeted labels and standards programmes. Energy efficiency labelling and standards programmes, when they are designed to facilitate rather than frustrate competition, can be effective in encouraging the development, marketing and sale of energy-efficient products. They can also re-enforce other policies to promote the use of energy-efficient products. They have already been used with some success for home appliances and office equipment. They are increasingly being considered for electric motors, home entertainment electronics, and lighting.

Labels and standards are generally designed to improve energy efficiency without degrading the products' other features: performance, quality, safety and overall cost. Much ex-ante analysis has been done to demonstrate their effectiveness in this regard. The programmes vary considerably among countries, because of differences in climate, consumers' product preferences and usage patterns, energy prices and product distribution channels.

This report presents the experience of existing labels and standards programmes in order to provide policy advisors and programme designers, managers and evaluators with:

- analytical and political support for current programmes,

- guidance and support for programmes under consideration or development,

- a basis for discussion of possible new international collaboration.

The report examines only the most prominent labels and standards programmes in IEA countries. It is not a comprehensive survey of programmes within the IEA or throughout the world.

TERMINOLOGY

Labels and standards include a variety of policy instruments that play different roles in government efforts to encourage the development, marketing and sale of energy efficient products.

Labels are markings, with supporting promotion and directories, which show products' energy use or efficiency according to a common measure. **Comparison labels** indicate the energy efficiency of a particular model relative to similar models on the market, and are usually, though not always, mandatory. **Endorsement labels** (or **quality marks**), affixed only on models meeting or exceeding a certain efficiency level, indicate by their presence models of superior energy efficiency. They are, by definition, voluntary. Ecolabels, not covered in this study, indicate multiple environmental parameters — such as noise, water use, and energy use — associated with the manufacture, use and disposal of products. Labels alert consumers to the energy use and costs of appliances and equipment, and enable the direct comparison of energy use or efficiency among different models.

Standards are mandatory programmes (regulations) stipulating the minimum efficiency levels or maximum energy-use levels acceptable for products sold in a particular country or region. They are often called minimum efficiency standards or minimum energy performance standards (MEPS). Though regulatory standards are most often applied to all products on a given market, the product coverage could conceivably be a given percentage of products on the market, a market-wide average or a manufacturer-based average. The U.S. Corporate Average Fuel Economy (CAFE) standards for automobiles are based on a manufacturer-based average. The minimum efficiency levels in regulatory standards are typically designed to lower the consumers' overall costs without compromising product performance and features. In some countries, standards are dictated by what is technically and economically feasible. In others, they are based on the mix of products in the marketplace at the time the standards were written. Regulatory standards are especially helpful in improving efficiency in cases where the purchaser and the end user are two different agents (frequently a landlord and a tenant), neither of whom pay the full cost of the product.

Targets are voluntary programmes in which governments or utilities persuade, but do not require, manufacturers to lower the energy use or raise the energy efficiency of their products. The product coverage can vary from all products on the market, to a given percentage of products on the market, to a market-wide average. They can also applied to manufacturer-based fleet averages or product category averages.

Though labels, standards and targets can be used individually with some effect, they are usually more effective when used together and in conjunction with other efficiency-promoting measures. These include information, education, financial incentives, targeted procurement, and research and development. For example, labels and directories can provide an information foundation for utility-based efficiency incentive programmes and government procurement directives.

In this report, the term "**labels and standards**" refers to the various types of labels, standards and targets and associated programmes collectively. The term "**refrigerator**" refers to refrigerators and to combination refrigerator-freezers.

CURRENT LABELS AND STANDARDS IN IEA COUNTRIES

Energy efficiency labels and standards are already widely used to improve the efficiency of home appliances and office equipment, and are increasingly being considered for electric motors, home entertainment electronics and lighting equipment. As of June 2000, energy-efficiency labels existed in 37 countries; standards in 34 countries (Table 1.1). This section gives brief descriptions of the most prominent programmes in IEA countries. Additional information is presented in Appendix 1.

Nearly all industrialised countries and many developing countries use labels for refrigerators and other home appliances. Many countries also have mandatory minimum energy-efficiency standards for refrigerators and room air conditioners. For other home appliances, minimum energy-efficiency standards are most used in Canada and the United States. Other countries use standards on a sporadic basis. Japan has standards for refrigerators and room air conditioners that specify lower limits for the average energy efficiency of each manufacturer's and importer's shipments in predefined product categories. Switzerland has used voluntary targets for refrigerators, clothes washing machines, clothes driers, dishwashers and electric ovens. The European Union has targets for clothes washers.

For office equipment and home electronics, endorsement labels are the most commonly employed energy-efficiency device. The European Group for Efficient Appliances (GEA) and Energy Star labels are used for personal computers, monitors, printers, copiers and fax machines. Regulatory standards are used only infrequently for such equipment. Japan has standards for televisions, videocassette recorders, photocopiers, computers and magnetic hard-disk drives. But voluntary targets or negotiated agreements are more common. Switzerland used voluntary targets for all major types of office equipment. The European Union has negotiated agreements for televisions, videocassette recorders and audio equipment.

Australia

As of June 2000, Australia uses labels and standards on the following products:

Labels and Standards	refrigerators and freezers
Labels only	clothes dryers; clothes washers; dishwashers; gas central heaters; gas space heaters; gas water heaters; and room air conditioners
Standards only	electric storage water heaters
Endorsement Labels	office equipment

The states of New South Wales and Victoria introduced Australia's first mandatory appliance labelling, for refrigerators, in 1986. By 1994, nearly all Australian states had put in place energy efficiency labelling for refrigerators, dishwashers, clothes washers, clothes dryers and room air conditioners making it a truly national programme (Harrington, 1997). Today, the labelling programme is co-ordinated at the national level. The Australian labels are category-type comparison labels, with the primary focus on ranking product models against a predetermined, open-ended efficiency scale (based on service per kWh). Secondarily, the labels indicate energy use (kWh per year) and performance, such as noise and cooling characteristics for refrigerators. The design and star rating algorithms of the labels have been recently reviewed to ensure their currency, usefulness to consumers and technical rigour. The new label (shown in Figure 1.1) will be launched in 2000. Australia has also adopted an endorsement labelling (Energy Star) programme for office equipment.

Gas water heaters, space heaters and central heaters are also labelled, under a separate programme administered by the Australian Gas Association. An extension of this programme is being examined for gas and electric cooking, and for electric storage, solar, and heat pump water heating systems.

The first minimum efficiency standards, for refrigerators and electric storage water heaters, were developed at the national level and took effect in October 1999. Additional standards for packaged air conditioners, lighting ballasts and motors have been proposed, but not yet authorised (NAEEEC, 1999).

Political support for labelling and standards was articulated in the 1998 National Greenhouse Strategy, which states that "improvements in the energy efficiency of domestic appliances and commercial and industrial equipment will be promoted by extending and enhancing the effectiveness of existing energy labelling and minimum energy performance standards programs". This is to be pursued by:

- developing minimum energy performance standards for a broader range of new appliances and equipment;
- regulating or developing codes of practice to ensure the adoption of energy performance standards;
- revising the technical framework of the labelling program to keep pace with improvements in product efficiencies including "super efficient" appliances;
- working with industry to improve gas appliance minimum energy performance standards and labelling programs; and

■ ensuring consistency of approach between Australia and New Zealand wherever possible

One planned action calls for Australia to match the world's "best practice" standards. In this regard, Australia will review the standards for high energy consuming appliances implemented by its major trading partners and then adopt the most stringent ones found. A review of refrigerator standards is already underway. Initial indications are that United States' 2001 standards will be become Australia's 2004 standards, with adjustments for climate, test procedures, and performance pre-requisites (Appliance Efficiency, 2000).

Table 1.1   Use of Labels, Standards and Targets Programmes for Major Home Appliances (as of June 2000)

	Number of Countries and EU		Countries and EU
	Labels	Standards or Targets	l = mandatory label; s = mandatory standard; t = target; vl = voluntary label; vs = voluntary standard
Refrigerators and Freezers			
IEA	8 + EU	6 + EU	Australia (l,s); Canada (l,s); European Union (l,s); Hungary (l,s); Japan (vl,s)*; New Zealand (vl); Norway (l); Switzerland (l,t); United States (l,vl,s)
Non-IEA	15	10	Brazil (l,vs); Bulgaria (l,s); China (s); Chinese Taipei (vl,s); Hong Kong China (vl); India (l,vs)*; Indonesia (vl)*; Iran (l,s); Korea (l,s)*; Lithuania (l); Mexico (l,vl,s); Philippines (l); Poland (l,s); Romania (l); Russia (s); Singapore (vl);* Thailand (vl)*
Clothes Washers			
IEA	7 + EU	4	Australia (l); Canada (l,s); European Union (l,vs); Hungary (l); New Zealand (vl); Norway (l); Switzerland (l,t); United States (l,vl,s)
Non-IEA	8	2	Bulgaria (l); China (s); Chinese Taipei (vl); Hong Kong China (vl); Lithuania (l); Mexico (l,s); Poland (l); Romania (l); Singapore (vl)

(continued)

Clothes Dryers			
IEA	6 + EU	3	Australia (l); Canada (l,s); European Union (l); Hungary (l); New Zealand (vl); Norway (l); Switzerland (l,t); United States (s)
Non-IEA	4	—	Bulgaria (l); Lithuania (l); Poland (l); Romania (l)
Dishwashers			
IEA	7 + EU	3	Australia (l); Canada (l,s); European Union (l); Hungary (l); New Zealand (vl); Norway (l); Switzerland (l,t); United States (l,vl,s)
Non-IEA	4	I	Bulgaria (l); Lithuania (l); Poland (l); Romania (l); Russia (s)
Room Air Conditioners			
IEA	5	3	Australia (l); Canada (l,s); Japan (vl,t,s); New Zealand (vl); United States (l,vl,s)
Non-IEA	8	8	Brazil (l); China (s); Chinese Taipei (vl,s); Hong Kong China (vl); India (vs); Korea (l,s); Mexico (l,vl,s); Philippines (l,s); Russia (s); Singapore (vl,s); Thailand (vl)
Electric Water Heaters			
IEA	2	3	Australia (s); Canada (s); New Zealand (vl); United States (l,s)
Non-IEA	—	3	Chinese Taipei (s); Mexico (s); Russia (s)
Lighting Equipment			
IEA	5 + EU	3	Canada (s); European Union (l); Hungary (l); Japan (l,s); Norway (l); Switzerland (l); United States (l,s)
Non-IEA	I I	5	Bulgaria (l); Chinese Taipei (vl,s); Hong Kong China (vl); Korea (l,s); Lithuania (l); Malaysia (s); Mexico (vl,s); Philippines (l,s); Poland (l); Romania (l); Singapore (vl); Thailand (vl)

Source: IEA
* Refrigerators refers to refrigerators and combination refrigerator-freezers.
** Applicable to refrigerators and refrigerator-freezers only, not stand-alone freezers.

Figure 1.1 Principle Energy Efficiency Labels Uses in IEA Countries

Australia

Canada

European Union

Japan

United States

United States

Group for Efficient Appliances (GEA)
Austria, Denmark, Finland, France, Germany,
The Netherlands, Sweden and Switzerland

Canada

Canada has an extensive appliance and equipment energy labelling and standards programme. As of June 2000, eight appliances are required to carry energy information labels, and twenty-eight products are required to meet minimum energy efficiency standards.

Labels and Standards	clothes dryers (electric, standard and compact); clothes washers; dishwashers; freezers; integrated stacking washer-dryers; ranges (electric); refrigerators; and room air conditioners.
Standards only	boilers (gas and oil); dehumidifiers; fluorescent lamp ballasts; furnaces (gas and oil); general service fluorescent lamps; general service incandescent reflector lamps; ground- or water-source heat pumps; ice-makers; internal water-loop heat pumps; large air conditioners, heat pumps and condensing units; motors (electric); packaged terminal air conditioners and heat pumps; ranges (gas); single-phase and three-phase single-package central air conditioners and heat pumps; single-phase and three-phase split-system central air conditioners and heat pumps; and water heaters (electric, gas and oil).

Canada introduced the world's first energy information label, the EnerGuide label, for refrigerators, in May 1978 (Figure 1.1). The EnerGuide labels are range-type comparison labels, with the primary focus on the numerical indication of the model's energy use or efficiency (Figure 1.1). Secondarily, the labels show the product's ranking on an energy use scale of all similar models available in Canada.

Provincial governments in Canada implemented minimum energy efficiency standards for equipment and appliances sold and leased in their jurisdictions as early as 1988. Federal-level standards were authorised in 1992, and first took effect in 1995. The programme expanded rapidly, with new standards taking effect for eighteen products in 1995, for two products in 1996, and for ten products at the end of 1998. Standards were increased for one product in 1997 and another product in 1998.

Czech Republic and Hungary

The Czech Republic and Hungary are among the ten Central and Eastern European (CEE) states that have announced their desire to join the European Union, and which have begun developing labelling and standards in line with the EU regulations as part of the accession process. The Czech Republic is currently preparing legislation that would adopt all of the EU labels and standards. In Hungary, energy labelling and standards of household electric refrigerators took effect in 1998, and labelling of clothes washers and dryers were implemented by December 1999. So far, three countries (Bulgaria, Hungary and Poland) have enacted legislation concerning both labelling and refrigerator standards; two other countries (Lithuania and Romania) have enacted just labelling legislation (Appliance Efficiency, 1999) (Dašek, 1999) (IEA, 1999).

European Union

Appliance labels and voluntary efficiency targets were used in the 1970s and 1980s in two individual European Union (EU) Member States, France and West Germany. In the 1990s, unilateral labels and standards programmes were proposed, but never implemented, in

Denmark and the Netherlands. The proposals did, however, prompt the European Commission to develop EU-wide programmes. As of June 2000, the EU requires labels on seven products, and has standards on two products and negotiated agreements on three products.

Labels and Standards	refrigerators; freezers
Labels only	clothes (tumble) dryers; clothes washers; clothes washer-dryers, dishwashers; and lamps
Standards only	hot-water boilers
Negotiated Agreements	clothes washers; televisions; videocassette recorders and audio equipment

The authority for all EU-wide energy labelling activities comes from a framework directive agreed to 1992.[1] The labelling specifications are spelled out in individual implementing directives for each product type. The first implementing directive, for refrigerators, was issued in January 1994 and took effect in January 1995. Labels only become mandatory in Member States when the governments have transposed the directives into national law. The EU labels are category-type comparison labels, with the primary focus on ranking the product models against a predetermined, open-ended efficiency scale (based on energy consumption [kWh] per year). Secondarily, the labels indicate energy use (kWh/year) and performance, such as noise and cooling characteristics for refrigerators (Figure 1.1).

There is no corresponding framework legislation giving the Commission the authority to introduce or revise efficiency standards on an on-going basis. Instead, each proposed standard

---

1. Council Directive 92/75/EEC of 22 September 1992 on the indication by labelling and standard product information of the consumption of energy and other resources by household appliances.

must be receive separate approval from the Council and the Parliament. There are currently EU-level minimum efficiency standards for two product classes — hot-water boilers and refrigerators. The standards for domestic gas- or oil-fired hot-water boilers took effect at the beginning of 1998; those for refrigerators took effect in September 1999. In June 1999, the Commission sent to the Parliament and Council a proposal for mandatory energy efficiency standards for fluorescent lighting ballasts. There have been studies and technical proposals for EU standards on other products, namely clothes washers, clothes dryers, dishwashers and air conditioners but none have been enacted.

In the future, the Commission intends to focus on negotiating agreements before developing additional regulatory standards (IEA 1994) (Waide, 1997). Thus far, negotiated agreements on four products have been concluded. An agreement with the European Federation of Domestic Appliance Manufacturers (CECED) on clothes washers was announced in October 1997. It seeks to improve the European average consumption of new models by 20 per cent (in relation to the new models of 1994) by the end of 2000, allowing for sales of higher consumption machines in Southern countries to be offset by the marketing of more efficient appliances in the Northern countries. In addition, the agreement contains some "soft targets" relating to certain features that may only be appropriate for certain groups of customers or regions, or which present particular marketing problems (Bertoldi, 1997) (Meli, 1997). Agreements have also been negotiated with European Association of Consumer Electronics Manufacturers (EACEM) to cut the power consumption of televisions, videocassette recorders and audio equipment when they are in standby mode (EWWE, 17 Oct 97). The Commission is continuing to pursue negotiated agreements on dishwashers, domestic electric storage water heaters, electric motors, external power supplies and set top boxes (Bertoldi, 1999) (Meli, 1999).

There have been task forces assessing the effects and feasibility of efficiency programmes on many other products, including air conditioners, motor systems end-use equipment (fans, pumps and compressors), office equipment and ovens.

Japan

The centrepiece of Japan's appliance and equipment efficiency programme is the Top-Runner standards scheme.

Top Runner — Standards and Endorsement Labels	passenger cars and trucks, air conditioners, refrigerators, fluorescent lights, televisions, videocassette recorders, photocopiers, computers and magnetic hard-disk drives

Japan's earliest "judgement" standards, product-weighted-average energy-efficiency targets, were set in 1979 for refrigerators and household air conditioners. Refrigerators met the targets in 1983, and were released (until recently) from further standards. Household air conditioners have been subject to successive targets since 1979. In 1993, new standards were established for heat pump air conditioners (dual use, heating and cooling), fluorescent lamps, televisions, photocopiers, computers and magnetic hard-disk drives to be met during 1998-2000. These standards have been replaced by the Top-Runner scheme, which sets the targets for the weighted-average energy efficiency of each manufacturer's and importer's shipments in predefined product categories to the level of the most energy-efficient model in each category on the current market. Today's best model sets tomorrow's standards. The targets range from 6.5% (of 1995 levels) to 83% (of 1997 levels) to be met by various years 2003-2010.

In Japan, manufacturers and importers of energy-consuming equipment are obliged to indicate the energy efficiency of their products. In addition, a voluntary labelling scheme will be introduced in the summer of 2000 for household appliances (Figure 1.1). These new labels indicate, with a symbolic mark, the product models' percentage fulfilment of the Top-Runner efficiency standards. MITI, by agreement with the U.S. Environmental Protection Agency, also uses the Energy Star endorsement label (Figure 1.1) for office equipment. The products concerned are personal computers, displays, printers, facsimile and copying machines, scanners, and multi-function devices. The Japanese and U.S. programmes maintain identical product specifications, and manufacturers which join one country's programme enjoy privileges in the other country's programme.

New Zealand

New Zealand's appliance and equipment efficiency programme includes labels (used on a voluntary basis), but no standards. There is one indigenous energy efficiency label for household appliances — on electric storage water heaters. However, product suppliers with interests on both sides of the Tasman Sea often leave Australian labels on their products sold in New Zealand. New Zealand has adopted the Australian energy label for refrigerators, dishwashers, clothes washers, clothes dryers, and room air conditioners on a voluntary basis (Cogan 1994). The labelling scheme is endorsed by the government, but run and managed by a third party. Though, New Zealand's Energy Efficiency and Conservation Authority (EECA) has been active in the joint (Australia and New Zealand) standards committees working on standards for refrigerators and electric storage water heaters, and has studied the feasibility of domestic standards for a range of household appliances, no such standards have actually been implemented.

Norway

Norway has implemented energy labelling for clothes (tumble) dryers, clothes washers, dishwashers, lamps, and refrigerators following the European Union directives on this matter (IEA, 1999).

Switzerland

In the 1990s, Switzerland used a system of target values with supporting endorsement labels to improve the energy efficiency of household appliances and the standby power use of home and office electronics equipment. The programme is currently being revised.

Target Values and Endorsement Labels	household appliances — clothes dryers, clothes washers, dishwashers, ovens, refrigerators, and freezers electronics equipment — fax machines, monitors, personal computers, photocopiers, printers, televisions, videocassette recorders

Energy matters in Switzerland have traditionally been the responsibility of the cantons and municipalities. In May 1991, after a constitutional amendment giving the Federal Government authority to carry out national energy policy, the Federal Office of Energy was charged with issuing requirements concerning the energy consumption of electrical appliances. Mandatory energy efficiency standards were not to be introduced unless appliances failed to meet certain energy consumption goals (target values) by set dates in the future. However, should the target values approach fail, mandatory standards could be imposed without seeking further political approval. Manufacturers were asked to reduce the energy consumption of their products to specified levels by given deadlines in the period 1996-2000. The target values and deadlines were fixed in collaboration with the manufacturers. The target value system did not set a standard which all models must satisfy but rather a target which applied to the average of the entire new sales weighted stock. The intention was that after the deadline 80-95 per cent of the devices sold, depending on the type of equipment, should use less energy than the target values.

The target value programme was complemented by the E2000 an endorsement label, which indicated models' energy consumption relative to a measure of progress towards the target. In 1999, Switzerland abandoned this label and adopted the Group for Efficient Appliances label (Figure 1.1).

Turkey

Turkey has not yet implemented labels and standards for appliances and equipment, but has a number of measures under consideration. A Working Group chaired by the National Energy Conservation Center (NECC) on the efficiency of household appliances and air-conditioners has been set up with participation from the private sector and public organisations concerned. Energy efficiency standards and regulations are in preparation for outdoor (street) lighting. Studies on the regulation of labelling for major domestic appliances have just been initiated by a sub-group that includes the representatives from General Directorate of Electrical Power Resources Survey and Development Administration (EIE), the Turkish Standards Institute, the Ministry of Industry and Trade and the Under-Secretary of Foreign Trade (IEA, 1999).

United States

The United States makes extensive use of comparison labels, endorsement labels and standards to improve the energy efficiency of electricity-, gas-, oil- and propane-using appliances and equipment.[2] As of June 2000, fourteen appliances are required to carry energy information labels, and twenty-five products are required to meet minimum energy efficiency standards. In addition, endorsement labels (Energy Star) are used for home and office electronic equipment, buildings and a variety of household products.

---

2. Water use labels and standards are applicable to showerheads, faucets, water closets (toilets) and urinals.

Comparison Labels and Standards	clothes washers; central air conditioners; dishwashers; fluorescent lamps and ballasts; compact fluorescent lamps; freezers; furnaces; general service incandescent lamps; instantaneous water heaters; heat pump water heaters; refrigerators; room air conditioners; swimming pool heaters; and water heaters
Standards only	central air conditioners heat pumps; clothes dryers; commercial furnaces and boilers; commercial packaged air conditioners and heat pumps; commercial water heaters; direct-fired space heaters; electric motors (1-200 hp); boilers; kitchen ranges and ovens;
Endorsement Labels	domestic appliances, heating and cooling equipment, home electronics, office equipment, lighting fixtures and bulbs, windows and buildings

Mandatory energy labelling of appliances and equipment was authorised in 1975, and the ensuing Energy-Guide programme took effect in May 1980. The Federal Trade Commission (FTC) developed and manages this programme. The Energy-Guide labels are range-type comparison labels, with the primary focus on the numerical indication of the product models' energy use or efficiency (Figure 1.1). Secondarily, the labels show the products' ranking on an energy use scale of all similar models available in the United States. They also show the estimated annual energy cost, based on the national average energy price.

The Energy Star programme combines an endorsement label (Figure 1.1) with information and promotion campaigns and alternative financing activities to improve energy efficiency (US EPA, 1998). The programme, begun in 1992, is a voluntary partnership of the Department of Energy (DOE), the Environmental Protection Agency (EPA), product manufacturers, distributors, utilities, energy-efficiency advocates, consumers, and other organisations. For the label, EPA and DOE work with manufacturers and other interested parties to establish energy-efficiency specifications for existing, proven technologies. Product models that exceed these specifications can be identified with the Energy Star label. For products subject to minimum efficiency standards, the models qualify for the Energy Star label if they exceed the standards by a certain amount, varying from product to product. Typically, the top quartile of models within a product class qualify for Energy Star. Other products, such as office equipment, the models qualify for the label if they have special features which enable them to use less energy than similar products.

The establishment of appliance standards in the United States took many years, and involved many organisations and numerous actions — some consensual, some confrontational — at both the federal and state levels. The earliest concrete proposals for efficiency standards were made California and the states in the northeast in the 1970s (before the first oil shock) in response to regional issues concerning the reliability of the electricity system and the environmental impacts of power plant siting. Federal appliance efficiency standards were first authorised in a voluntary form in 1975 and then made mandatory in 1978. However, it was not until 1988 that efficiency standards for most major types of residential energy equipment were established. The first standards of consequence — for refrigerators, freezers, room air conditioners and water heaters — took effect in January 1990. Apart from a temporary moratorium during 1995-96, the standards have been, and continue to be, updated and strengthened regularly.

North American Co-ordination — NAFTA

Canada and the United States have been quite active in the area of harmonisation. Many of the efficiency standard levels are the same as well as many of the test procedures. More recently, partially as a result of the North American Free Trade Agreement (NAFTA), Canada, Mexico and the United States have entered into negotiations to harmonise test protocols for certain appliances. This may lead to greater harmonisation of labels and standards requirements also. At this time there are no official agreements between the countries. The Canada, Mexico and the United States already use the same test procedure for refrigerators, room air conditioners and motors. Mexico is not yet testing the appliances though.

Pacific Rim Co-ordination — APEC

There are currently investigations under way within Asia Pacific Economic Cooperation (APEC), of which Australia, Canada, Japan, New Zealand and the United States are members, to assess the feasibility of mutual recognition of laboratories and harmonising test protocols, labelling and efficiency standards. This is being undertaken by the Energy Working Group of APEC, Energy Efficiency and Conservation Experts Group.

POLICY PRIMER: STEP-BY-STEP GUIDE TO PROGRAMME DEVELOPMENT AND IMPLEMENTATION

INTRODUCTION

Labels, standards and targets programmes are developed and implemented differently throughout the world. However, there are some underlying elements that are fairly common to all of them. This chapter describes these elements in the form of a generalised step-by-step guide to programme development and implementation with a view to thorough consideration of the numerous interests and issues involved. It focuses on labels and standards in the context of a package of market transformation interventions.

It should be understood from the outset that the process described is an idealised one. It portrays policymaking that takes place in an open, transparent manner — where the interests of all stakeholders are fully considered — with adequate time and resources to thoroughly analyse and deliberate all the relevant issues. While policymaking does not always take place in such an environment, the step-by-step guide can still give guidance as to the required elements for a successful programme.

There are seven basic steps to developing labels, standards and targets programmes.
1. Preliminary Assessment and Priority Setting
2. Authorisation and Programme Design Procedures
3. Priority Refinement — Products and Instruments
4. Design — Technical Parameters and Compliance Deadlines

5. Design — Testing Procedures

6. Design — Administrative Rules and Conformity Assessment

7. Monitoring, Evaluation and Reporting

These steps are not necessarily sequential. In many cases they will be taken simultaneously. The principal tasks, considerations and goals associated with each step are described below.

STEP 1 — PRELIMINARY ASSESSMENT AND PRIORITY SETTING

This step encompasses the preliminary consideration of technologies, markets and policy instruments with a view to securing political authority for the programme from the parliament, head of government or other authority. Strong political authority, based on a law or executive decree, is not only necessary for establishing the legality of some interventions, but is vital to eliciting constructive input and co-operation from stakeholders during the programme design phases.

Most of the work of this stage involves the preliminary assessments — via analysis and stakeholder consultation — of the engineering, market, economic impact and policy situations (Table 2.1). These assessments are used to develop initial priorities concerning products and policy measures.[3] A priori conclusions favouring certain products and interventions should be avoided. Investment in good, solid analysis at this stage pays off in greater credibility in consultations and negotiations with stakeholders. And attention to stakeholder concerns at this point will help make the proposed programme more attractive to ministers, and will aid in building consensus in later stages.

---

3. Note that more in-depth engineering, market and economic impact assessments are undertaken in Steps 3 and 4.

Table 2.1 Tasks, Considerations and Goals of Preliminary Assessment and Priority Setting

Tasks	Considerations	Overall Goals
Engineering and market assessments — preliminary analysis and stakeholder consultations. (Note that more in-depth assessments are undertaken in Step 3)	■ Product energy use characteristics and trends, including expected efficiency improvements absent market transformation intervention ■ Pace of product technology change ■ Level of potential energy savings and CO_2 reductions through improved product efficiency ■ Cost-effectiveness of energy savings and CO_2 reductions through improved product efficiency, as measured by life-cycle costs and payback periods ■ Market structure and stakeholders ■ Technical and market barriers slowing the development and dissemination of more efficient products in the existing market	■ Well articulated goals of market interventions: (such as: meeting climate change mitigation commitments; addressing other energy system and environmental concerns; providing support for other policy measures; countering adverse effects of interventions taken by trading partners; reducing friction among state, provincial or local interventions; protecting consumer interests) ■ Strategic plan for market intervention, specifying: – preliminary product priorities – general rationale for level of proposed interventions – envisioned market roles of favoured interventions in furthering the development, diffusion and implementation of energy efficient technologies – preliminary matching of interventions with products (priorities should be based on the engineering, market, economic impact and policy assessments, not on a priori conclusions)
Economic impact assessment — preliminary analysis and stakeholder consultations. (Note that a more in-depth assessments is undertaken in Step 4)	■ Assess the impacts of possible interventions on local manufacturers, distributors, retailers, consumers and utilities, in terms of production costs, investment recovery, profitability, competition effects, product availability, life-cycle costs , payback periods, etc. ■ Examine the various roles of market actors in the technology development, diffusion and implementation process in order to identify programme-enhancing collaboration and partnership opportunities	
Policy assessment — analysis and stakeholder consultations.	Identification of full spectrum of market transformation interventions, and assessing each as to its: ■ technical and market feasibility, in terms of realisable energy savings and CO_2 reductions, costs to stakeholders and administrative burden to government	

(continued)

	■ need for new or revised testing procedures ■ potential roles in addressing technical and market barriers slowing the development and deployment of more efficient products in existing market ■ political viability, in terms of stakeholder support and consistency with the market intervention preferences of political leadership ■ contributions to non-energy objectives, such as economic development, employment, trade, building comfort, consumer amenity, and health and safety ■ coherence with: – other government policies (energy and non-energy) – utility programmes and other private initiatives – policies of trading partners and state, provincial and local governments (with attention to pressures to co-ordinate or harmonise interventions)	■ Recommendations for provisions of a framework law or decree, such as: – defined objectives – authorised type of intervention (labels, standards, targets, etc.) – general criteria for product coverage – general level of technical intervention (expressed in terms such as consumer payback period, life cycle costing criteria, world class challenge or harmonisation with trading partners) – envisioned timeframe – rulemaking process and deadlines – expected programme impact reports ■ Heightened awareness among stakeholders of impending policy intervention
Assessment of international co-operation	Consider usefulness and feasibility of international co-operation in various aspect of the market transformation intervention, including design, execution and evaluation	
Report to Parliament, Head of Government or other authority	Present the case for authorisation of market transformation intervention, via legislation, decree, executive order as necessary	

The findings of these assessments should be summarised in a report to the Parliament, Head of Government or other authority. The report should outline the justification for the proposed market interventions, and should contain draft provisions that could be written directly into the law or decree. The draft provisions should be as technically explicit as possible in order to make the law or decree clear and unambiguous. They should describe the objectives, criteria for product coverage, deadlines, rulemaking procedures and expected programme impact reports for each proposed intervention.

It is especially important that the draft provisions be clear about intended level of ambitiousness of the interventions. Are the measures intended to improve product efficiency by a certain amount? or make the products incorporate all energy saving features with a certain consumer payback period? or help make domestic industry a world leader in manufacturing efficient products? or make product requirements comparable to those of trading partners? Decisions concerning this general level of technical intervention will heavily influence the remainder of the programme development process.

STEP 2 — AUTHORISATION AND PROGRAMME DESIGN PROCEDURES

As mentioned earlier, the controversy that frequently surrounds the proposals for labels, standards and targets programmes, if left unresolved, can be detrimental to the design and operation of the programme. It is therefore important to deal with potential issues as early and as thoroughly as possible. An important step is to establish strong and clear political authority for standards.

Political authority can come from various sources depending on the nature of the governments involved. It is strongest when it is widely recognised as a reflection of social consensus, supported by top political leaders, and if possible, articulated in binding *framework law or decree* with *jurisdictional legitimacy,* accompanied by *practical support for programme development and operation.* Whatever the form of expression, political authorities should establish a clear sense of:

- the strength of their political resolve,

- the objectives,

- the lines of programme authority,

- the boundaries for programme intervention,

- the need for an open and transparent process for programme design, and

- the relationships with other relevant energy and non-energy policies.

Japan, for example, faced the domestic situation to take stricter measures to achieve the Kyoto commitments. The Top Runner Program, the stricter energy efficiency standard, was introduced in 1999 and revised into the Law Concerning Rational Use of Energy (known as the Energy Conservation Law). During this revision, the target of the efficiency was decided in a short time. These actions were influenced by the political pressure of the coalition ruling parties, the initiative of the Prime Minister as well as other concerned ministers. It was widely supported by the nation.

Framework Law or Decree

The political authority for labels, standards and targets should be grounded on a strong, but flexible foundation. In most countries, this means enacting a framework law or issuing a decree that calls for interventions for certain products, with provisions for expanding and revising the programme later. The nature of the law or decree depends in large part on the political consensus required for its approval. For example, if there exists a solid, yet possibly fleeting, consensus, it may be advisable to act quickly and outline only the basic framework of the programme in the law itself. The technical details could be left to a regulatory or other administrative body. If on the other hand, there were more time and extra work needed to build a consensus, it may be advisable to engage interested parties to write the technical details into the law itself.[4]

At the very least, framework legislation or decree should provide:

- defined programme objectives,

- authorised type of intervention (labels, standards, and/or targets),

- general criteria for product coverage,

- expected levels of technical intervention (based on consumer payback time, life cycle costing criteria, world class challenge, or harmonisation with trading partners),

- envisioned implementation timeframe,

- process rules and deadlines, and

- expected programme impact evaluation reports.

The amount of technical detail (product categories, standards levels, implementation dates, revision schedules, etc.) specified in the law or decree is a matter of strategy. More detail in the enacting legislation adds strength to the political legitimacy, but may inhibit the process of political consensus. Political consensus is very delicate with respect to timing. If the analytical work necessary to establish the technical details is not completed at the time when political consensus for the principal of intervention is reached, it may be best to act promptly with a less technical framework law or decree.

The United States provides a good of example of these types of issues. The federal standards program was contested bitterly in its

---

4. Details concerning test protocols probably should not, however, be written directly into the law. The procedure of revising test protocols, which is necessary from time to time, does not warrant rewriting the law. It is best if the law simply reference test protocols written by other parties.

early stages. Initial federal legislation mandating that standards be developed by a regulatory agency (the Department of Energy) was unsuccessful in actually getting standards implemented. Implementation came only after additional legislation, containing specific technical details, was enacted.

Of course, the problem of technical detail is made easier if there are existing international "model" technical specifications (relevant to the market in question) that can be referenced in the framework legislation or decree.

Jurisdictional Legitimacy

An important element of political authority is an accord between the products and geography to be influenced and the jurisdiction of the particular government doing the intervening. For the sake of programme effectiveness and economies of scale, governments may prefer to intervene in as large a market as possible. But in fact, they may not hold the authority to act at such levels. The issues can be especially complex in federated states. The national-level government may or may not have sufficient authority to regulate or other influence all the types of commerce involved.

The case of Canada is a good example. In Canada, federal jurisdiction with respect to energy is limited to international and inter-provincial commerce. Thus, the federal standards apply only to products imported into Canada and/or shipped between provinces, and not to products manufactured and sold within a single province. Given the nature of the Canadian appliance and equipment market, this jurisdiction is sufficient for an effective programme. Standards apply to the vast majority of products sold in Canada.

Australia is another example. Individual states and territories are responsible for legislation, regulation and associated administration. State-based legislation is necessary because the Australian constitution gives Australian states clear responsibility for resource management issues, including energy. Thus the role of the federal government has become one of co-ordination. Federal authorities assist in writing "model" legislation that the states and territories then "mirror."

Practical Support for Programme Development and Operation

It should be recognised that labels, standards and targets must evolve with the products and their markets. Otherwise, there could be missed opportunities for substantial energy savings and carbon emission reductions. There could also be risks of unintended obstructions to product development.

The programmes should thus be revised and updated on a regular basis. For standards, this can require a great deal of additional analysis concerning the viability and cost-effectiveness of standards. The process can be another source of controversy. For example, in the United States, standards development was delayed for a year or so during 1995-96 because of stakeholder discontent with the process of standards revisions. It is necessary to establish a process of revision that minimises the non-substantive issues of disagreement, and allows full consideration of substantive issues. In the U.S. case, the programme got back on track only after an extensive reform of the process gave stakeholders a say in each step of the revision process — from priority setting to final rulemaking.

Lastly, it should not be forgotten that the development, maintenance, operation, and evaluation of programmes require resources. Substantive negotiations on the technical details of interventions cannot take place without good technical data and analysis and periodic programme evaluation. Well designed framework laws or decrees and procedural rules cannot be followed if they are not accompanied by adequate funding.

Table 2.2   Tasks, Considerations and Goals of Authorisation and Programme Design Procedures

Tasks	Considerations	Overall Goals

Programme authorisation — in the form of a framework law or decree	Framework law or decree should, to the extent possible, specify:
	■ Overall programme objectives
	■ Authorised types of intervention (consistent with jurisdictional authority)
	  – Instruments (labels, standards, targets, etc.)
	  – Market transactions (all domestic production, imports, inter-provincial trade, etc.)
	■ General criteria for product coverage
	■ General level of technical intervention (in terms of consumer payback time, life cycle costing criteria, world class challenge, domestic top runner challenge, harmonisation with trading partners, etc.)
	■ Envisioned timeframe
	■ Rulemaking processes and deadlines
	■ Expected programme impact evaluation reports
		■ Political legitimacy for energy-efficiency initiatives through demonstrated strength of political support and resolve
		■ Clear programme objectives and boundaries
		■ Clear lines of programme authority
		■ Open and transparent process for programme design
		■ Planning for coherent relationships with other relevant energy and non-energy policies

Budget for programme development and administration		

STEP 3 — PRODUCT PRIORITY REFINEMENT

This step encompasses analytical and stakeholder consultation activities to further refine the product priorities established in Steps 1 and 2. Once established, the refined product priorities should be set forth in a multi-year work plan for the programme.

The engineering and market assessments are essentially in-depth versions of those conducted in Step 1. They are the basis upon which the order of product interventions in the multi-year plan are scheduled. Products may be given high or low priority for early action for various reasons, including the amount and cost of realisable energy savings and CO_2 reductions, product development cycles, etc.

This priority setting activity should not be viewed as a one-time only exercise. It should be conducted on a periodic basis in order to stay current with changing product developments, market situations and programme resource levels. In the United States, for example, it is an annual exercise.

Table 2.3   Tasks, Considerations and Goals of Product Priority Refinement

Tasks	Considerations	Overall Goals
Engineering and market assessment — full analysis and stakeholder consultations.	In-depth examination of same factors and considerations listed in Table 2.1, with additional consideration to: ■ the technical, economic and market potential for energy savings and CO_2 reductions for major product types (taking into account the capabilities of local and foreign manufacturers, existing and emerging market situations, etc.) ■ the sensitivity of results to varying energy prices within jurisdiction ■ methods for defining, measuring and comparing product energy use, performance and duty cycles ■ baseline forecasts of product purchases, product use rates, energy use, energy efficiency and CO_2 emissions for use in later programme impact evaluations	■ A multi-year work plan, reflecting – refined product priorities – timetable for programme review and updates ■ Baseline forecasts of product purchases, product use rates, energy use, energy efficiency and CO_2 emissions for later evaluation efforts
Assessment of data system	Assess data collection and processing needs, and their compatibility with existing systems	
International co-operation	Seek international co-operation in programme areas identified in Step 1 as useful and feasible	

STEP 4 — DESIGN — TECHNICAL PARAMETERS AND COMPLIANCE DEADLINES

This step involves setting the technical parameters and deadlines for the high-priority products identified in Step 3. The technical parameters are standards set points and labelling algorithms. These parameters are discussed at length in Chapter 3. The deadlines should be consistent with manufacturing adaptation times, as determined by product development cycles and production line changeover schedules.

*Table 2.4   Tasks, Considerations and Goals of Design —
Technical Parameters and Compliance Deadlines*

Tasks	Considerations	Overall Goals
Announce process for developing product-specific interventions	■ Encourage stakeholder participation in drafting technical parameters ■ Facilitate consensus building among stakeholders	■ A set of technical parameters for each product chosen for intervention. Technical parameters should be: – be realistic with respect to existing and forecasted market profiles – be realistic with respect to compliance deadlines – be consistent with the general degree of technical intervention set out in the framework legislation or decree) – balance comprehensiveness, thoroughness and simplicity – avoid giving incentives that favour use of higher energy use product models – avoid technological lock-in
Economic impact assessment — full analysis and stakeholder consultations	In-depth examination of same factors and considerations listed in Table 2.1, with additional consideration to: ■ sensitivity of results to varying energy prices and monetary currencies within jurisdiction	■ A label design that it is clear, informative and attention-getting

(continued)

Define product-specific technical parameters (with as much stakeholder consensus as possible)	■ Define standards set points
	■ Define labelling algorithms
	■ Define compliance deadlines, consistent with:
	  – technical parameters and adaptation time (based on product development cycles and production line changeover schedules)
	  – product availability disruption
	  – inventory clearing	

Design labels	Design visual format of labels, and market test proposed designs to check consumer understanding and responsiveness	
Design adjunct programmes	Design promotion, education, sales person training and fiscal elements of labelling programme	

The technical parameters and deadlines should be based on the engineering and market assessments conducted in Step 3, an in-depth economic impact assessment and extensive stakeholder consultations. In some cases, stakeholder groups can actually take the lead role in negotiating and writing the technical parameters and deadlines. If the group is reasonably representative of the principle stakeholders — manufacturers, consumer advocates, utilities and environmental interest groups — efforts should be made to facilitate their constructive interaction, and high priority should be given to their recommendations.

It is important that the members of the stakeholders group have fairly similar view of the intended ambition of the intervention. This is one reason why the framework law or decree should be as explicit as possible in this regard.

STEP 5 — DESIGN — TESTING PROCEDURES

Energy use test protocols, standard methods for measuring of products' energy use, are the cornerstone upon which all labels, standards and target programmes are built. They are necessary for making information comparisons (labels) and compliance claims (standards and targets) meaningful. Test protocols are very technical in nature, typically specifying: 1) energy use metrics, such as kWh/day, 2) product operating cycles and conditions under which energy use measurements are made, such as ambient and working temperature for refrigerators or water hardness and detergent types for clothes washers, 3) performance metrics, 4) model categories, such as the star system for rating the cooling ability of freezers, 5) electricity input voltages and frequencies, 6) allowable tolerances and 7) measuring instrument specifications. Because of the technical details involved, and the desire for consensus in the development process, test protocols frequently take three or more years to develop.

Governments usually relinquish the responsibility for developing and maintaining test protocols to trade associations or national, regional or international standards organisations. The International Organization for Standardization (ISO) and the International Electrotechnical Commission (IEC) are the two primary international standards setting organisations for appliances and equipment. The ISO has developed energy use test protocols for refrigerators and air conditioners; the IEC has developed tests for wet appliances and microwave ovens. Neither has developed protocols to measure the energy use of office equipment, nor have they issued ratings guides, labels, regulatory standards or targets pertaining to the energy efficiency of appliances or equipment.

An ISO/IEC standard may be used as published, or may be implemented through incorporation in national standards of different countries. However, there is no binding obligation for affiliate standards institutes to adopt ISO standards or for manufacturers in

ISO affiliate states to test their appliances according to ISO test and measurement standards. The European Union and Australia require that their test protocols be based on ISO/IEC test procedures.

In many instances the protocols for measuring the energy efficiency of appliances and equipment are not codified by the standards institutions until governments ask for tests to support their proposed ratings, labels, targets, and codes programmes. This does not imply, however, that the tests are non-existent prior to their codification by standards organisations. Some tests are developed in manufacturer or professional associations, and are not recognised as official standards until the need arises. For example, the US refrigerator/freezer test protocol was based on American Society of Heating, Refrigerating and Air Conditioning Engineers (ASHRAE) tests.

*Table 2.5   Tasks, Considerations and Goals of Design —
Testing Procedures*

Tasks	Considerations	Overall Goals
Select or develop test protocols	In consultation with national and international standards organisations and other stakeholders, select (adapt) or develop test protocols, specifying: ■ energy use metrics ■ product operating cycles and conditions ■ performance metrics ■ model categories ■ electricity input voltages and frequencies ■ allowable tolerances ■ measuring instrument specifications.	Test procedures that: ■ give accurate and reproducible data on energy use and performance for a wide range of product models and duty cycles ■ are low cost ■ are easily adaptable to new product technologies or features ■ do not act as barriers to trade

STEP 6 — DESIGN — ADMINISTRATIVE RULES AND CONFORMITY ASSESSMENT

Conformity assessment refers to the procedures by which products are evaluated and determined to conform to labelling and standards rules. In other words, it is the system for checking whether products are displaying the required labels, whether the labels are truthful and whether the products are meeting the required standards. The function of the conformity assessment system is to ensure the credibility of labels and standards programmes by maintaining the confidence of manufacturers, customers and other market participants in the programmes.

The conformity assessment system encompasses various measures taken by manufacturers, regulatory authorities and independent, third parties. It can include sampling and testing, certification and quality system assessment and registration. It also includes accreditation of the competence of those activities by a third party, and recognition (usually by a government agency) of an accreditation programme's capability (NRC, 1995) (Breitenberg, 1997) (ISO, 1991). The *sampling and testing* may be done by manufacturers and/or independent laboratories. A *manufacturer's declaration of conformity* is the assessment by the manufacturer based on internal testing and quality assurance mechanisms. *Independent laboratories* may also test products as a service to manufacturers. This may be used to confirm manufacturers' tests, or may be used by small manufacturers not having in-house testing capabilities, or may be required by regulation. *Certification* is the formal verification by an un-biased third party, through testing and other means, that a product conforms to standards and/or is labelled truthfully. It is by definition exclusively a third party activity. *Quality system registration*, is the result of an independent audit and approval of the manufacturer's quality control system. This helps to strengthen confidence in the presumption that test results on a sample of a manufacturer's product are valid for all the products shipped. *Accreditation*, defined as a procedure by which an authoritative body gives formal recognition that a body or person is competent to carry out specific tasks (ISO/IEC), is most commonly applied to laboratories in the context of labels and standards programmes. It refers to the process of evaluating testing facilities for competence to perform specific tests using standard test methods. In addition to these features, conformity assessment systems may have mutual recognition provisions. Mutual recognition refers agreements between conformity assessment entities (in different countries, for example) to accept some or all aspects of one another's work. A mutual recognition agreement between two countries would mean that a particular product would need to be tested and certified in only one of countries, but could be sold in both countries. This reduces testing costs and administrative expenses.

Table 2.6   Tasks, Considerations and Goals of Design —
Administrative Rules and Conformity Assessment

Tasks	Considerations	Overall Goals
Conformity assessment procedures	Design conformity assessment system, with: ■ certification procedures, whether by independent laboratories or manufacturer self-declaration ■ data reporting rules, processing procedures and public access rights ■ monitoring and verification procedures — spot checking or sampling programme ■ compliance enforcement and sanctions mechanisms ■ dispute mechanisms ■ mutual recognition agreements with foreign conformity assessment systems	■ Solid programme credibility through the proof that rules are being followed ■ Data and procedures to provide assurance of programme conformance, and to allow credible, low-cost assessment of the programme's impact ■ Administration procedures that are simple, clear and transparent, with low costs to government and stakeholders ■ Laboratory accreditation procedures that have low costs and do not act as barriers to trade
Laboratory accreditation	■ Identify or develop accreditation scheme for certifying the competence of independent laboratories (or manufacturers themselves) to carry out necessary tests	
Data support for programme impact evaluation	■ Data collected during conformity assessment can be used in the general programme impact evaluation, and should made collected in such a way as to maximise its usefulness for this purpose, while maintaining necessary confidentiality	

STEP 7 — MONITORING, EVALUATION AND REPORTING

Rigorous and routine monitoring, evaluation and reporting is vital to ensuring the effectiveness of, and political confidence in, any public policy. Monitoring and evaluation helps improve the operation, management, oversight and planning of these instruments by promoting transparency and realism of goals, enhancing financial and managerial accountability, highlighting progress towards goals, and identifying barriers to success. These issues are becoming increasingly important because of tighter constraints on public budgets, greater demands for political accountability and increased pressures of international commitments. Performance measurement and evaluation enable politicians, policy professionals, programme managers and staff, and taxpayers to ascertain whether programmes are meeting objectives and public money is being well spent. In the case of energy efficiency, these stakeholders need to know whether energy efficiency programmes have resulted in improved energy efficiency, energy savings and/or reduced greenhouse gas (GHG) emissions and whether the programmes might be improved and savings increased.

*Table 2.7   Tasks, Considerations and Goals of Monitoring,
Evaluation and Reporting*

Tasks	Considerations	Overall Goals
Monitor market for compliance and progress towards targets	Monitor whether: ■ Products are tested according to prescribed protocols and certified compliant as required ■ Test results are reported to proper authorities ■ Energy and performance values reported on labels are truthful ■ Products being sold meet or exceed prescribed standards ■ Laboratories are being accredited properly	■ Solid credibility through public accountability for programmes' accomplishments ■ A programme that is cost-effective and relevant in the face of technological development and market trends ■ Low evaluation costs ■ Data on the impact of programmes for analytical forecasts
Stakeholder consultation and market trend monitoring	■ Keep alert to programme problems and issues, ■ Watch for problems and opportunities that may be suitable for intervention	
Programme evaluation	Conduct regular evaluations of the programme's: ■ Market impacts ■ Energy savings and CO_2 reductions ■ Consumer and manufacturer costs ■ Administration costs ■ Administration effectiveness	
Report programme results	■ Report programme results to political authority and public as required by framework legislation and general principles for open and transparent governance	
Review and revise programme baseline forecasts	■ Review and revise (if necessary) baseline forecasts of product purchases, product use rates, energy use, energy efficiency and CO_2 emissions, and feed into analytical forecasts	

LESSONS LEARNED AND EXAMPLES OF GOOD PRACTICES

INTRODUCTION

Labels, standards and other market transformation activities,[5] seek to increase the production and use of more energy-efficient products. To be successful, these instruments must be implemented in a manner that takes account of the great complexity of the technology development, diffusion and implementation process, and that exhibits a high degree of market and political credibility. This chapter presents some general principles of policy development and examples of good practices that derive from this complexity and need for credibility.

COHERENT PACKAGES OF MULTIPLE POLICY INSTRUMENTS

To be successful in improving products' energy efficiency, labels, standards and other market transformation activities must take account of the great complexity of the technology development, diffusion and implementation process. Part of the complexity derives from the multifaceted nature of improving the production and use of more energy-efficient products, as highlighted in the schematic of

---

5. *Market transformation refers to a system of intentional actions to shift markets in terms of product availability and customer choice. It implies a greater consumer or demand-side influence on the development and dissemination of technology. It encompasses actions aimed at equipment performance (both stand-alone and in systems), market dissemination of products and actors' orientation towards new products. In the energy efficiency context, market transformation aims to shift away from products with inferior energy use patterns by moving improved products to market faster and widening their share of the market (IEA, 1997). Many different instruments are being tried in order to attain the desired changes, for example, labelling schemes, rebate programmes, minimum efficiency standards, information, education and various types of procurement programmes (Engleryd, 1998).*

product efficiency and market penetration (Figure 3.1). There are various ways to improve the product-market profile, including:

(a) encouraging the purchase of higher efficiency products,

(b) discouraging the purchase of low efficiency products and

(c) encouraging the production and marketing of products more efficient than currently available.

The multiple market objectives mean that no single policy instrument can realistically be expected to deliver all the potential cost-effective savings for a given product. It is necessary to implement coherent packages of multiple policy instruments, making sure that the component instruments complement and reinforce, and avoid contradicting, each other.

Labels and standards each play different roles in encouraging the development, marketing and purchase of energy efficient products (Box 3.1). Labels, for example, can be expected to make *some* customers less likely to choose the market's poorest performing products, but is not likely to eliminate those products from the market completely. Also, labels do little to discourage landlords from furnishing apartments with cheaper, less-efficient products when tenants pay the utility bills. And most standards, while removing the poorest performing products from the market, do little to encourage the development of still more efficient products. Given the various goals to be achieved, policymakers should think in terms of coherent packages of multiple policy instruments, making sure that each of the component instruments complement and reinforce, and avoid contradicting, each other to the extent possible.

It should also be noted that at larger geographical levels, especially at the international level, the complexity — in terms of product types and market situations, the actors and their relationships with each other, and the political and social authority of various actors to intervene — is greater still. This can make developing a single, uniform package of policy measures for the entire region very difficult.

*Figure 3.1 Impact of Several Market Transformation Instruments
on the Dissemination of Energy Efficient Equipment*

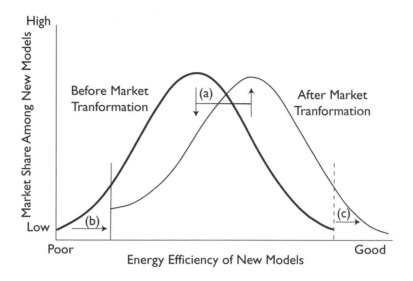

(a) Labels, fiscal incentives and other customer focus instruments increase the average efficiency of the market, increasing the market shares of efficient models at the expense of inefficient ones. Also, fleet average standards and voluntary programmes encourage manufacturers to increase the average efficiency of their product lines.

(b) Minimum efficiency standards prevent the marketing of low-efficiency appliances. This process is facilitated on markets where labels have already reduced the market shares of the products.

(c) Support for innovation and research and development, enable new, more efficient, products to be introduced to the market.

Note: This diagram is a stylised representation of the market profile. The relative sizes of the market transformations (a), (b) and (c) can vary considerably. The market transformations also have time and cost elements, which are not shown.

Sources: Laponche, 1997 and NRCan, 1998.

Box 3.1   *Market Roles of Ratings, Labels, Standards and Targets*

Energy efficiency labels, standards and targets play different, but complementary, roles in the appliance and equipment markets.

Labels, and closely-related ratings systems, alert and inform consumers to the energy use, energy costs and environmental consequences of their purchase decisions. They also protect consumers from inaccurate claims concerning these attributes made by manufacturers and dealers. The thinking is that energy and environmental characteristics are invisible, but important product attributes about which consumers need to be given explicit information in order to make more rational purchasing decisions. And when given accurate and reliable information, customers are more likely to factor energy costs and/or environmental concerns into their decisions, and to purchase products that have lower overall costs (typically being more energy efficient) than they would otherwise. The energy use and cost information, which is far less apparent than the purchase price, can be considered as a second price tag. Labels also provide an information foundation for other energy efficiency measures, such as utility efficiency incentive programmes and procurement initiatives. In turn, by raising energy's profile in the appearance of products and influencing consumer buying decisions, labels signal to manufacturers the need to develop, produce, and market more efficient products.

Regulatory **standards** prevent manufacturers from placing products on the market that fail to meet certain minimum efficiency levels. They require manufacturers to raise the efficiency of their below-standard models, find other markets for them, or cease to produce them. The minimum efficiency levels in standards are typically set at levels that lower the consumers' overall costs without compromising product performance and features. Standards, therefore, make rudimentary trade-offs between purchase costs and operating costs for consumers. This embedded (invisible) trade off is especially helpful when the purchasers and end user are different entities, such as a landlords and tenants, where neither party pays the full cost of the product. The fact that the trade off is embedded (and thus never lost) is also effective in improving the efficiency of used products, where labels and other sources of running cost information are usually available.

Targets directly inform manufacturers that governments, and frequently consumer and environmental advocates, want to see products of certain efficiency levels offered and promoted in the marketplace. Usually, targets are aimed at:
1) raising the average efficiency of total sales of a product to a specific level, or
2) introducing new, more efficient products to the market.

Though ratings, labels, targets, and regulatory standards can be used individually with some effect, they are usually more effective when used together and in conjunction with other efficiency-promoting measures such as information, education, financial incentives, targeted procurement, and research and development.

The process of discussion and negotiation of labels, standards and targets is also a key part of the information and communication process in the market. It helps government policymakers and public interest advocates communicate to manufacturers and others in the supply chain society's preferences concerning energy efficient products. In the other direction, it helps communicate knowledge about the technical and economic feasibility of more efficient products and systems.

One example of a comprehensive market transformation effort is the motor systems efficiency programme in the United States. The U.S. DOE supplements the legislated motor standards with its Motor Challenge programme to change other important aspects of the market. The Motor Challenge programme seeks to harness market forces and commercial interests to promote motor system efficiency via energy-efficient motors, drives and driven equipment (e.g. pumps and fans) as well as motor systems integration and optimisation. Its mechanisms include an Information Clearinghouse providing data on the practicality and profitability of electric motor system strategies; design-decision tools such as motor systems database software; Showcase Demonstration projects; and training, workshops and conferences. The programme works within existing market structures and makes heavy use of partnerships with commercial interests, such as equipment manufacturers, distributors, users and other companies.

Another example is the European Commission's SAVE programme, which has implemented a mix of labelling and classification schemes, minimum efficiency standards, negotiated agreements and technology procurement to transform the market for equipment in the domestic, commercial and industrial sectors. In the residential sector, the programme elements include:

■ *Labels* for refrigerators, clothes washers and dryers, dishwashers, ovens and lamps. Labels for electric water heaters and room air conditioners will be finalised during 2000.

■ *Label promotion and information activities* to improve the effectiveness of labels. The responsibility for increasing the public's awareness and understanding of the labels lies with the public authorities (at the national and local levels), utilities and retailers. For its part, the Commission is conducting pilot projects on increasing consumer awareness and training retail staff.

■ *Minimum efficiency standards* for refrigerators. The standards are closely linked to the labels, with the maximum allowable energy for most models set to about the level dividing the C and

D label categories, thus excluding the majority of D, E, F and G refrigerators from sale.

■ *Negotiated agreements* on clothes washers and consumer electronics. The agreement on clothes washers is also linked to the labelling scheme. The first stage, starting on 1 January 1998, phased-out of clothes washers in the label classes F, E and G; the second stage, beginning on 1 January 2001, will remove machines in class D having spin speeds greater than 600 rpm and capacities greater than 3 Kg from the market. Other negotiated agreements, with consumer electronics manufacturers, seek to reduce the standby losses of televisions, video cassette recorders (VCRs) and audio equipment. A negotiated agreement for dishwashers is under consideration.

■ *Technology procurement* aimed at improving the higher, more efficient end of the market. A project called Energy+ involves ten national energy agencies running an EU-wide co-operative procurement of highly efficient refrigerators. The goal is to create a market for appliances using less than three-quarters of the energy of equivalent class A appliances. Under the project, participating retailers and institutional buyers declare their intention to promote and/or purchase appliances meeting the Energy+ specifications.

■ *Design competition*, with marketing and promotion of winning designs, to development and market attractive dedicated CFL fixtures (Bertoldi, 1999).

OPEN, TRANSPARENT AND SYSTEMATIC PROGRAMME DEVELOPMENT PROCEDURES

The complex product and market goals described in the previous section demand rigorous priority setting in the development of labels, standards and associated programmes. There are far more combinations and policy instruments than can be implemented at once. Priorities must be set with due consideration for the:

- level of cost-effective energy-saving potential for products
- trends in product design and product line cycles — when can new energy efficiency features be taken on with minimal marginal cost and disruption?
- trends in technology development — are there major technological developments on the horizon that could benefit from early energy efficiency intervention?
- pace of technology development — is the technology changing at pace where interventions could contribute lasting change?[6]
- component make-up of products — are the components, such as motors and power supplies, more amenable to intervention than the products themselves?
- existence of up-to-date testing protocols
- types of measures trading partners are taking
- amount of additional analysis needed
- the ease with which consensus among stakeholders could be achieved.

Two tasks are indispensable in assessing these issues and developing credible, workable priorities: (1) stakeholder consultation and consensus and (2) market and engineering analysis. It is also important that these exercises by carried out in an open, transparent and predictable manner. This helps ensure that programmes are developed in a manner consistent with technical, economic and commercial realities. It also increases the likelihood that stakeholders will support the programme.

---

6. Some technologies change so quickly that administratively heavy measures risk being obsolete by the time they are actually implemented.

Stakeholder Consultation and Consensus

There is great diversity of the actors involved — consumers, manufacturers, distributors, retailers, architects, contractors, trades people, professional societies, utilities, consumer advocates, environmental interest groups, government, etc. — in labels, standards and other market transformation activities. Each stakeholder has different interests, or more precisely, each actor trades-off energy efficiency with a different set of concerns. For example, manufacturers must weigh the marginal costs and revenues of enhancing the energy efficiency of their products against those of developing some other feature, product or even business. And customers must weigh the effort of consciously researching and considering the energy aspects of their purchases against the energy cost savings resulting from that effort. Moreover, there is diversity within the various groups of stakeholders themselves. Individuals make decisions according to their own personal situations and values. They adopt new technologies at differing rates, from early adopters to laggards. And they react differently to various stimuli — published information, independent ratings and recommendations, voluntary commitments, mandatory rules, taxes, rebates — when making technology decisions.

The diverse interests of these many stakeholders can be a source of policy conflict. Labels and standards, when first proposed, are almost by definition contentious. They compel someone to do something they would rather not, and there is uncertainty that they will yield significant results.[7] For example, standards compel industry to design, manufacture and market more efficient products than they would otherwise. The controversy varies by instrument. Standards,

---

7. In fact, there are at least three interests that will often contest some aspect of labels, standards and targets. First, there are the manufacturers, distributors and retailers, for whom the instruments represent added cost, inconvenience, and reduced technology and marketing choice. Second, there are public interest advocates, who frequently question the adequacy of particular instruments in addressing the issues at hand. Third, there are people who oppose some instruments (in particular regulatory standards) on ideological grounds — that they are not appropriate or effective instruments for accomplishing social goals.

because of their costs, are most controversial for industry; targets, because of their uncertainty, are most controversial for environmental advocates. Labels tend to be the least controversial of the three, but they do entail testing costs, administrative inconvenience and reduced energy marketing discretion to manufacturers, and there is sometimes controversy about whether they influence consumer behaviour or not. Regardless, such controversy, left unresolved, can be detrimental to the design and operation of an effective product efficiency programme. It is therefore important to deal with potential issues as early and as thoroughly as possible, by establishing strong and clear political legitimacy for programmes and by encouraging consensus among stakeholders.

In this regard, experience from many countries has shown that effective programmes are difficult to establish without stakeholder involvement. At a minimum, there needs to be an open and transparent way for stakeholders to make their concerns known, and some method to ensure that substantive concerns will be addressed. At the next level, the stakeholders might also be included in the priority setting and analytical stages of the programme development process. And if possible, attempts should be made to engender trust between stakeholders. Once trust is established, it is easier to conduct good faith negotiations, concentrating on issues of legitimate disagreement and hopefully producing better programmes. A good example is the Canadian programme, which at the outset put ample emphasis on stakeholder consultation, resulting in minimum controversy and little resistance from manufacturers.

Some lessons can also be drawn from the U.S. programme. Stakeholder discontent with the standards revision process in the United States in 1995-96 led extensive reform of the process. The U.S. Department of Energy recently revamped its system for setting and revising standards with the help of many stakeholders. The new procedural guidelines are published in *Procedures, Interpretations and Policies for Consideration of New or Revised Energy Conservation Standards for Consumer Products*, July 1996. The major objectives of the new rules fall into three categories:

Procedural — provide for early input from stakeholders; increase the predictability of the rulemaking timetable; reduce the time and cost of developing standards.

Analytical — increase the use of outside expertise; eliminate design options early in the process; conduct thorough analyses of impacts; use transparent and robust analytical methods.

Interpretive — fully consider non-regulatory approaches; articulate policies to guide the selection of standards; support efforts to build consensus on standards (Miller, 1997).

In this regard, following good policy consultation procedures is essential. Consultation is an important element of market communication, helping to convey the energy efficiency preferences among various parties. Consultation among diverse stakeholders might also be a source of policy creativity. That is, it could lead to new and better policy measures to address energy efficiency issues in real market situations. It is the IEA's hope that international information exchange, and publications such as this one, can also foster such policy creativity and diffusion.

Engineering and Market Analyses

Engineering and market analyses are other vital elements to developing programmes with the right balance of impacts and costs. Since such analyses are expensive and time consuming, it is important that they be conducted systematically, according to clear, but flexible guidelines. The goals should be timeliness and comprehensiveness to avoid overlooking opportunities, and realism with respect to different technical and market situations. To maintain an adequate degree of comprehensiveness, while keeping analytical costs low, the priority setting should be structured to recognise and screen out less viable options from further consideration sooner rather than later.

In the United States, the law authorising standards and its accompanying procedural rules set out explicit guidelines for developing and revising standards. First, product design options are screened for:

- Technological feasibility
- Practicability to manufacture, install and service
- Adverse impacts on product utility or product availability
- Adverse impacts on health or safety.

Then an engineering analysis is conducted to determine the likely cost and performance improvement of each of the candidate design options. From this efficiency/cost relationship, measures such as payback, life-cycle cost, and energy savings are developed and cost efficiency curves are constructed.

Afterwards, in the market analysis, candidate standards are assessed as to their:

- *Manufacturer impacts*, including: estimated impacts on cash flow; assessment of impacts on manufacturers of specific categories of products and small manufacturers; assessment of impacts on manufacturers of multiple product-specific Federal regulatory requirements, including efficiency standards for other products and regulations of other agencies; and impact on manufacturing capacity, plant closures, and loss of capital investment.

- *Consumer impacts*, including: estimated impacts on consumers based on national average energy prices and energy usage; assessments of impacts on subgroups of consumers based on major regional differences in usage or energy prices and significant variations in installation costs or performance;

sensitivity analyses using high and low discount rates and high and low energy price forecasts; consideration of changes to product utility and other impacts of likely concern to all or some consumers, based to the extent practicable on direct input from consumers; estimated life-cycle cost with sensitivity analysis; and consideration of the increased first cost to consumers and the time required for energy cost savings to pay back these first costs.

■ *Competition impacts.*

■ *Utility impacts*, including: estimated marginal impacts on electric and gas utility costs and revenues.

■ *Energy, economic and employment impacts*, including: estimated energy savings by fuel type; estimated net present value of benefits to all consumers; and estimates of the direct and indirect impacts on employment by appliance manufacturers, relevant service industries, energy suppliers and the economy in general.

■ *Environment and energy security impacts*, including: estimated impacts on emissions of carbon and relevant criteria pollutants, impacts on pollution control costs, and impacts on oil use.

■ *Impacts relative to non-regulatory approaches*, including: the impacts of market forces and existing voluntary programs in promoting product efficiency, usage and related characteristics in the absence of updated efficiency standards.

The engineering, manufacturer impact and consumer impact analyses are described more fully in Appendix 2.

While the analytical burden inherent in these rules is more appropriate for engineering/economic-based standards than for statistically-based standards, the main elements deserve consideration in all programmes.

Systematic Process for Integrating Stakeholder Interests and Analytical Findings

It is important that the stakeholder consultations and the engineering and market analyses are carried out in a systematic manner. A well-planned process aids in the integration of the two elements and the development of strong programme.

The U.S. programme provides a good example of a very methodical programme development process. Table 3.1 outlines the process, showing the key methodological and analytical issues to be considered at each stage.

Table 3.1   Outline of U.S. Standards Setting Process, as revised in 1996

Stages and Primary Inputs (•) and Outputs (⇨)	Factors Considered
PRIORITY SETTING • Preliminary Analysis • Stakeholder Consultation of Draft Agenda ⇨ Regulatory Agenda — annual publication of rulemaking priorities and accompanying analysis and schedules for all priority rulemakings anticipated within the next two years	Potential energy savings and economic, environmental and energy security benefits; applicable rulemaking deadlines; incremental U.S. DOE resources required to complete the rulemaking; other regulatory actions affecting products; stakeholder recommendations; evidence of energy efficiency gains in the market absent new or revised standards; status of required changes to test procedures; and other relevant factors.
DESIGN OPTION SCREENING[8] • Expert and Stakeholder Consultation ⇨ Identification of product categories and design options to be analysed further, or to be eliminated from further consideration ⇨ Identification of key issues and expertise necessary to conduct further analysis ⇨ Identification of any needed modifications to test procedures	Technological feasibility; practicability to manufacture, install and service; adverse impacts on product utility or product availability; and adverse impacts on health or safety. (Note: initial criteria for screening according to these factors are written directly into the rules, e.g., design options not incorporated in commercial products or in working prototypes will not be considered further, nor shall design options having significant adverse impacts on the utility of the product to significant subgroups of consumers).

ENGINEERING REVIEW • Engineering Analysis — to establish the likely cost and performance improvement of each design option • Expert and Stakeholder Consultation ⇨ Candidate Standards — Advance Notice of Proposed Regulation (ANOPR), specifying candidate standards, but not proposing a particular standard ⇨ Technical Support Document (TSD)	Excluding design options that do not meet the screening criteria or that have payback periods greater than the average life of the product, the candidate standard levels will typically include: the most energy- efficient combination of design options, the combination of design options with the lowest life-cycle cost, and combination of design options with a payback period of not more than three years.
ECONOMIC IMPACT REVIEW • Economic Impact Analysis — impacts on manufacturers, consumers, competition, utilities, non-regulatory approaches,[9] environment and energy security, and the national energy, economic and employment situation • Public Comments and Stakeholder Negotiation • Stakeholder Review ⇨ Proposed Standards — Notice of Proposed Regulation (NOPR) ⇨ Final Technical Support Document (TSD)	A high priority is placed on consensus stakeholder recommendations and supporting analysis.[10] Principles for the analysis of the impacts on manufacturers (in terms of costs, sales, net cash flow, etc.) and consumers (in terms of product availability, first costs, payback period, etc.) are written directly into the rules. Analytical assumptions are specified for crosscutting factors, such as economic growth, energy prices, discount rates, and product-specific energy efficiency trends absent new standards.
STANDARD SETTING • Final Public Comments and Stakeholder Negotiation ⇨ Final Standards	Standards must meet statutory requirements, i.e., be technologically feasible and economically justified, likely to result in significant energy conservation, not likely to result in the unavailability of any covered product type with performance characteristics (including reliability), features, sizes, capacities and volumes generally available in the U.S. at the time.

8. Design options, which figure prominently throughout the engineering analysis, refer to alternative component technologies and configurations for the products in question. For example, the design options examined in the 1995 Technical Support Document on refrigerator standards included: increased insulation thickness for walls and doors; increased resistivity of insulation; improved gaskets, different anti-sweat and defrost technologies; different compressor, condenser, evaporator and valve technologies; and alternative refrigerants.

9. The rules place a high priority on non-regulatory approaches, stating that non-regulatory approaches are valuable complements to the standards program. In particular, voluntary programmes are to be considered where it appears that highly efficient products can obtain a significant market share but less efficient products cannot be eliminated altogether.

10. If a joint stakeholder group provides analyses, addressing all of the statutory criteria and using valid economic assumptions and analytical methods, the U.S. DOE is expected to use this supporting analysis as the basis for the proposed rule. Such recommendations are considered most valuable if the group is reasonably representative of the principal stakeholders, including manufacturers, consumers, utilities, states and representatives of environmental or energy efficiency interest groups.

PROGRAMME ELEMENTS THAT REFLECT PRODUCT AND MARKET REALITIES

The principle programme elements — test protocol, labels, and standards — should be designed so that they fit the markets in which they will function. They should be as simple as possible, while taking due account of product and market complexities.

Test Protocols

Energy use test protocols, the standardised methods for measuring of products' energy use, are the cornerstone upon which all labels, standards and target programmes are built. They are necessary for making information comparisons (labels) and compliance claims (standards and targets) meaningful.

For each general product type, there are often hundreds of models on the market. Each model offers a different package of service, in terms of "non-energy" performance, features and quality. Since the purpose of labels and standards is not to diminish product service, the test protocols and programmes need to be tailored to the many different combinations of service on the market. The most common way is to segment the market according to two analytical constructs — a performance metric and model categories. The *performance metric* is comprised of: 1) the principle performance measure, such as litres of cooling space for refrigerators or kilograms of clean clothes for clothes washers and, as needed, 2) a definition of quality of the performance, such as "clean" clothes and dishes for clothes washers and dishwashers, and 3) adjustments to account for technical efficiencies that vary with the principle performance measure, such as the tendency for refrigerator efficiency (in terms of kWh per litre of cooled adjusted volume) to improve with increasing size, and 4) adjustments to account for special features, such as automatic defrost. *Model categories* are used to account for discrete differences in models, such as refrigerator/freezers with the freezer on top vs. the freezer on the bottom. The number of product categories used should represent a balance of the needs for simplicity and having each category represent reasonably uniform functionality. These service parameters are usually, if not always, set out in a way intended to not penalise products for using additional energy for providing additional performance and features.

As mentioned in Chapter 2, test protocols are very technical in nature. They spell out in detail: 1) energy use metrics, such as kWh/day, 2) product operating cycles and conditions under which energy use measurements are made, such as ambient and working temperature for refrigerators or water hardness and detergent types for clothes washers, 3) performance metrics, 4) model categories, such as the star system for rating the cooling ability of freezers, 5) electricity input voltages and frequencies, 6) allowable tolerances and 7) measuring instrument specifications. Because of the technical details involved, and the desire for consensus in the development process, test protocols frequently take three or more years to develop. An ideal test would:

- reflect actual usage conditions;
- yield repeatable, accurate results;
- accurately reflect the relative performance of different design options for a given appliance;
- cover a wide range of models within that category of appliance;
- be inexpensive;
- be easy to modify to accommodate new technologies or features;
- produce results that can be easily compared with results from other test procedures.

As these goals are in part contradictory, all energy test protocols are necessarily compromises. A test that aims to reproduce actual product usage conditions will probably be expensive and difficult to replicate. At a minimum, however, tests should rank different models' energy use in the same order as would be expected under field use conditions (Meier, 1997b).

It is difficult and often time consuming to develop test procedures that are simple and robust. They must be specific and detailed enough to give reasonably accurate and reproducible results, without wasting time and effort on excessive measurement precision. Three main factors guide the development of protocols for measuring the energy use of a products: 1) simplicity, 2) reproducibility, and 3) representativeness of actual operating conditions. Of course, representativeness embodies a great deal uncertainty about climate, operating conditions, equipment options and human behaviour, and can be a major challenge to achieve across wide geographical and cultural areas. For example, given general climatic variations and kitchen temperature variations, there is no "right" ambient refrigerator temperature. Another example, illustrating the complexity of capturing actual operating conditions through test procedures and communicating the variability of the results is a typical U.S. automobile fuel economy sticker (Box 2.1). Given the possible variations, test protocols should describe a limited range of approximate, yet realistic, conditions under which energy use measurements are to be made. Retaining a fair degree of closeness between tests and actual operating conditions, requires creativity in writing test procedures.

Box 2.1   Typical U.S. Automobile Fuel Economy label

City 25   Highway 33   MPG (miles per gallon)

Actual mileage will vary, with options, driving conditions, driving habits and vehicle condition. Results reported to E.P.A. indicate that the majority of vehicles with these estimates will achieve between 21 and 29 mpg in the city, 28 and 38 on the highway. Estimated Annual Fuel Cost $643.

Because one of the goals is usually to keep the system as simple as possible (for comprehension by manufacturers and users) countries concentrate on those traits most relevant to their own markets. The categorisation schemes mirror to a great extent the product preferences of the various countries and regions. For example, there are many refrigerators in the United States with side-by-side refrigeration and freezer compartments, so the standards categories recognise this layout. By contrast, these style of refrigerator is not widespread in Europe, so the EU's label scheme takes no account of them. In practice, no attempt to group appliances into categories for energy efficiency evaluation will ever be ideal.

Europe, Japan, and North America use different testing protocols for most products. Europe tends to adopt the testing protocols developed by the ISO and IEC. In part, this is because of Europe's large influence in these organisations, which means that international test protocols tend to address European concerns. Because of the close integration of the North American economies, Canada, the United States, and increasingly Mexico use similar, and often equivalent, test protocols. For microwave ovens, most countries have adopted the international test protocol (IEC 705).

Table 3.2 shows some of the values of the main test parameters for refrigerators/freezers, clothes washers, clothes driers, and dishwashers. Among the parameters which vary among the test protocols are: 1) input voltage and frequency (not shown in table); 2) energy efficiency metric; 3) air temperature and humidity conditions; 4) water temperatures; 5) usage assumptions; 6) energy efficiency credits or debits for special features; and 7) performance specifications and measurements. Performance aspects are the most difficult to agree upon, manufacturers and testing agencies often have different approaches to measuring the performance of dishwashers and clothes washers.

Table 3.2   Principal Characteristics of Test Protocols for Home
Appliances.

	ISO/IEC (Europe and Japan)	Australia & New Zealand	Canada & United States
Refrigerators			
Ambient Temperature (°C)	25	32	32.2
Fresh Food Temperature (°C)	5	3.3	3.3,7.2
Freezer Temperature (°C)	−6,−12,−18	−9	−9.4,−15, −17.8 (freezer only)
Door Openings	No	No	No
Loading	Yes	Energy (No), Performance (Yes)	No
Clothes Washers			
Wash Temperature (°C)	90 & 60 (60 & 40)	min. 35, also cold at 20 proposed	60
Usage (cycles/week)			8.0
Remaining moisture credit	No	No	No
Performance measure	Yes	Yes, multiple	No
Energy use metric	kWh/kg		ft^3/kWh
Clothes Dryers			
Auto termination credit	No	No	Yes
Usage (cycles/week)			8.0
Performance measure	Yes	Yes, multiple	No
Energy use metric	KWh/kg	kWh/kg moisture removed	kWh/lb
Dish Washers			
Inlet Water Temperature (°C)	15	20	49
Wash Temperature (°C)	65	65	60
Usage (cycles/week)	4.0	7.0	6.2
Performance measure	Yes	Yes	No
Loaded/Soil	Yes/Yes	Yes/Yes	Yes/No
Energy use metric	kWh/setting	kWh/yr	cycle/kWh

Source: Turiel, 1995

Information Label Algorithms and Design

The purposes of information labels are to alert and inform consumers about the energy use and costs of their prospective product purchases, protect consumers from inaccurate claims made by manufacturers and dealers, and provide an information foundation for other energy efficiency measures (Box 3-1). At a minimum, information labels should provide two services. They should draw increased attention to energy vis-a-vis more apparent product attributes, such as size, colour and purchase price. They should also portray accurate information that is easily compared among product models. To do this, labels must be visually striking, convey information quickly and Intuitively, be supported by promotion efforts and salesperson training to increase recognition and understanding.

The basis of the labelling programme is the labelling algorithm, the overall system of model categories, performance metrics, energy use metric and categories, sensitivity parameters and revision schedules. The algorithm should be developed in close conjunction with the test protocols. The model categories and performance metrics should developed such that like is compared with like to the extent possible.

The revision schedule is a very important part of the labelling algorithm. The addition of new models and the discontinuance of old models will over time affect the usefulness of the various categories and reference points. Revisions need to be timed in a manner that balances stability with up-to-date market representation. Stability means that labels should not change so frequently that it is common to find two models, manufactured only a short time apart, with different labelling parameters. On the other hand, the endpoints and categories should always be fairly representative of the products on the current market.

Most information labels rely on some sort of graphic to draw attention and to convey information quickly and memorably. There are three general approaches to these graphics — one based on the range of efficiencies of the product models available, another based on pre-defined efficiency categories and the last based on progress towards a target level. Canada and the United States use the range method; the European Union and Australia use the category method; and Japan will be using the target method (Figure 3.2).

Figure 3.2 Example of Canadian (Range) and European Union (Category) Labels

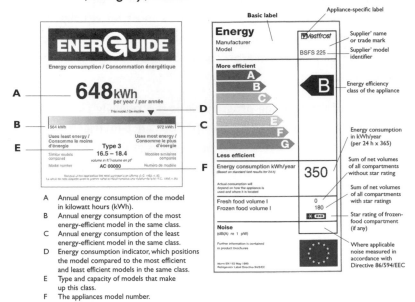

A   Annual energy consumption of the model in kilowatt hours (kWh).
B   Annual energy consumption of the most energy-efficient model in the same class.
C   Annual energy consumption of the least energy-efficient model in the same class.
D   Energy consumption indicator, which positions the model compared to the most efficient and least efficient models in the same class.
E   Type and capacity of models that make up this class.
F   The appliances model number.

Range labels

Range labels use a linear graphic to show how the energy use or efficiency of the model in question compares with the most-efficient and least-efficient models on the market. The endpoints of the scale show the efficiency range of the market; the pointer represents where the particular model falls in that market range.

A potentially confusing aspect of range labels is that the scale ranges can vary considerably across model categories. For example, in the United States in 1999, one category of refrigerator (with a top-mounted freezer) had a market range of 526 to 741 kWh/year (a range of 215 kWh/year, or 34 per cent of the median), another category (identical, except for a side-mounted freezer) had a market range of 710 to 783 kWh/year (a range of 73 kWh/year, or 10 per cent of the median).[11] This type of situation forces consumers — at least the ones perceptive enough to notice — to make decisions as to whether the scale range itself is significant enough to be concerned about, and about how to compare ranges across model categories.

An important issue with range labels is how frequently the endpoints of the scale are revised to reflect models leaving and entering the market. One option would be continuous revisions, that is labels are changed whenever a new most/least efficient model enters the market or an old most/least efficient model leaves the market. This approach guarantees that all new labels are current, but risks confusion for older labels and is administratively burdensome. Imagine, for example, being in a store and seeing product models having different scales simply because they were labelled just before and just after a new most efficient model came on the market. Another option is to make the revisions on a regular basis, such as 6 months or a year. The approach works well except when a new most/least efficient model enters the market in mid-period. In such a case, the model efficiency would be outside of the range supposedly on the market. The United States and Canada use the latter option. The ranges are recalculated annually, and are revised only if the endpoints change by 15 per cent or more from those previously published range. Product labels prior to the revision are not required to be relabelled. In the case where a model falls outside

---

11. The model categories were both 18.5 to 20.4 cubic foot refrigerators with automatic defrost and without through-the-door ice service. The only difference was the placement of the freezer section.

the published range, the pointer is omitted from the scale and a sentence stating that "the estimated annual energy consumption (or energy efficiency rating) of this model was not available at the time range was published" is added to the label.

Category labels

Categories labels show energy use or efficiency according to pre-defined ranking categories. The width of the categories can vary in order to show a reasonable degree of differentiation in the products. The categories should be defined such that there is a fairly even distribution of models falling into the middle and poorer grades (to offer a basis for differentiation) and relatively fewer models falling into the better grades (to challenge manufacturers to build better models). The categories on the European Union's label refer to ranges of an energy efficiency index — the ratio of the appliance's energy consumption to a standard energy consumption defined in the establishing directive (EU Directive 94/2/EC). The index ranges are 55 or less (category A), 55-75 (B), 75-90 (C), 90-100 (D), 100-110 (E), 110-125 (F) and 125 or greater (G). The indexes were defined such that the average European appliance when the labels were established had an index of 100, and thus fell at the dividing line between the D and E categories (Winward, 1998). Australian labels use a similar system, with a scale of stars representing ranges of service/kWh.

Because the categories are pre-defined and stretch beyond the efficiency levels found on the current market, category labels do not require frequent endpoint revisions. However, the fact that the labels do not give an indication of the current market situation is a drawback. The label does not show how far the model in question is from the best and worst models available. Nor do they show how good or bad the best and worst models are. Thus, for example, some consumers may spend time looking for a top category appliance, only to find out later that no appliances have actually attained that level yet. Of course, this information can be discovered from product listings or from salespersons, but the label itself does not indicate it.

Category labels need revision from time to time, but certainly less frequently than do range labels. Revision is required when, and if, the market evolves in a manner such that nearly all models cluster in too few categories. If this happens, the category system gives consumers little useful information upon which to chose one model over another. At that time, the categories should be recalibrated, in terms of the placement of the average product model and the width of the category ranges. As at the beginning of the programme, there should be a fairly even distribution of models falling into the middle and poorer grades (to offer a basis for differentiation) and relatively fewer models falling into the better grades (to challenge manufacturers). Such a large change, should be indicated clearly on the label so that consumers do not attempt a direct comparison between old and new labels.

Category labels have the advantage of being easier to understand and not dwelling on small differences in efficiency levels. Also, category labels can fit well with a standards or target programme. Standards can be expressed in terms of the set point that divides any two of the categories. Models in categories lower than the set point could be banned from the market. Or models in categories higher than the set point could be part of an purchasing incentive programme.

For both range and category labels, considerable care should be given to clear indication of which end of the range or categories represent the most efficient, lowest energy cost models, and which represent the least efficient models. Market research has shown that this has been a source of confusion for some labels.

Target labels

Japan will introduce a voluntary labelling scheme as part of the Top-Runner programme in the summer of 2000. These new labels will use symbolic marks to indicate the ratio (on a percentage basis) between a particular product model's energy efficiency and the targeted Top Runner efficiency level. This will enable consumers to compare the energy efficiency among many products in a relative and quantitative way. The scheme can maintain the effectiveness of the provided information, taking into account the improvement of the energy efficiency in products each year.

Standards Set Points

There are two basic analytical approaches to establishing energy set points for standards and targets, one based on statistical methods, the other on engineering/economics methods. In the statistical approach, the energy efficiency levels of all product models on the market are evaluated, and the set points are established at levels that eliminate a certain portion of the least efficient models. In the engineering/economics approach, the costs of improving the efficiency of a particular product (via various design options) are assessed, and the standards or targets are established at levels deemed to technologically feasible and economically justified, though possibly not met by any models on the market. Often, the statistical method is used when targets and standards are first introduced, and the engineering/ economics method is used to update and modify the standards and targets. The statistical approach has the advantage of being less data intensive and thus less expensive and quicker to carry out. The engineering/ economic method, on the other hand, can support the development and adoption of more stringent efficiency levels. The United States uses the engineering/economics method; Canada uses the statistical method; the European Union used the statistical approach with its refrigerator standards; Japan's Top Runner is a special case of the statistical approach where the set points are set at the level of the best products on the current market.

Figure 3.3 illustrates these two different approaches to standards setting. The U.S. 1990 standard (solid line) was obtained through a consensus approach between manufacturers and environmental groups; the net result of that approach is to eliminate about half of the models available in 1989. In that consensus approach, current data on refrigerator models was used to establish a minimum performance standard that was adopted by the U.S. Congress in 1987 and became effective in 1990. The engineering/economic approach was used to develop the 1993 standards. It can be seen that when the 1993 standard was established in 1989, that there were no top-mount auto-defrost refrigerator models that met the 1993 standard. A statistical approach could never produce such a result as was obtained for the 1993 standards. The statistical approach however, has the advantage of being carried out much more quickly than the engineering/economic methodology. All that are required are current energy efficiency data on existing models of the appliance in question (Turiel, 1995).

Figure 3.3 Efficiency Gains with Standards in the United States (for top-mount auto-defrost refrigerators)

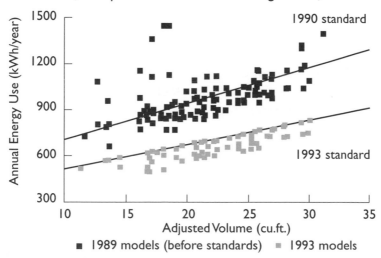

■ 1989 models (before standards)   ▪ 1993 models

Sources: LBNL, 1995

Another important aspect of set points concerns their application. In most cases, they are stated as minimum efficiency levels or maximum energy use levels that must be met by all products models on the market. In other cases, notably Switzerland's targets and the United States' Corporate Average Fuel Economy (CAFE) standards, the set points refer to efficiency levels that must be met by the weighted average of all models on the market. In the case of Japan's Top Runner standards, the set points refer to efficiency levels that must be met by the weighted average in each product category. This approach allows less efficient models on the market as long as they are offset with enough high-efficiency models.

SOLID PROGRAMME CREDIBILITY

Labels and standards must exhibit a high degree of market and political credibility. For the programmes to work well, it is essential that market actors and political interests have confidence that they are working well. There are two elements to this confidence — that among programme participants and that among the public, their government representatives and the programme personnel.

First, manufacturers must believe that their products (and their competitors' products) will be held firmly to the labelling and standards rules. Otherwise, the incentives for cheating are not offset by probable detection and penalties. Likewise, for labelling programmes, consumers need to believe that the information presented is accurate. Otherwise, there is no incentive for considering the information. It is the function of the conformity assessment system described below to assure this market confidence in the programme.

Second, the public and their government representatives must have confidence that the programmes are accomplishing what they set out to do, within the budgets allocated to them. This is vital for programme continuity, which in turn is necessary for sustained market transformation. Programmes that do not meet their goals within their budgets will sooner or later be subject to additional political scrutiny. This may result in revisions towards more realistic programme goals and budgets, but it may also call into question the political consensus underlying the programme, ultimately risking programme discontinuation. It is the function of the programme monitoring, evaluation and reporting system described below to instil confidence in the public and political authorities that the programme is on track. Monitoring and evaluation systems also helps keep programme personnel accountable, and provides early feedback on programme problems and opportunities.

Conformity Assessment and Enforcement

The role of conformity assessment and enforcement systems is to maintain the credibility of labels and standards programmes among stakeholders. They encourage manufacturers to represent their products truthfully, thus inspiring consumers to believe the information on product labels and trust that the products themselves meet applicable standards.

The inherent level of compliance and trust varies among cultures, so it can be expected that conformity assessment and enforcement systems will differ also. What is important is that such systems encompass levels of testing, reporting and checking that achieve the right balance of programme credibility and costs, keeping in mind that as product trade increases, the systems will need to gain the understanding and confidence of trading partners as well as domestic participants. It is also important that the systems are presented in a manner in which all programme participants understand their responsibilities. Though many stakeholders are involved, monitoring compliance and undertaking enforcement actions if non-compliance is detected is primarily a government responsibility.

As described in Chapter 2, there are many features to a conformity assessment system, including product sampling and testing, conformity declaration, certification, quality control assessment, and accreditation.

An example of a coherent and well articulated compliance and enforcement policy is found in Canada. Natural Resources Canada publishes its *Compliance Policy for the Energy Efficiency Act and the Energy Efficiency Regulations* to set out the principles of a "fair, predictable and consistent approach to enforcement" (NRCan, 1995). The document is intended as guidelines for regulators in carrying out their compliance and enforcement actions, and as an aid for regulatees in understanding the measures that the regulator will use to ensure compliance with the law. Briefly, it explains the purpose and requirements of the law on labels and standards, the philosophy of the compliance system, the activities undertaken to monitor compliance, and the enforcement actions undertaken in cases of non-compliance.

One interesting aspect of the system, is its commitment "to achieving a high level of voluntary compliance."

"NRCan believes that a high level of voluntary compliance is most likely to occur when all parties affected by the Act and the Regulations support them. This philosophy is reflected in the approach that was used to develop the Act and Regulations and will be continued as their key operating principles in their administration. These operating principles are: 1) consulting stakeholders, 2) minimising regulatory burden, 3) harmonising with other jurisdictions, 4) co-operating with key players and 5) informing regulatees and the public."

The Guide states very clearly and concisely what is required of dealers (manufacturers, importers, sellers and lessors):

■ import or ship between provinces, only energy-using products that meet energy-efficiency requirements;

■ ensure that customs documents contain complete information about an energy-using product;

■ ensure that an EnerGuide label is on the products that require labels before their first sale or lease;

- ensure that energy-efficiency verification mark from an accredited certification organisation is on the an energy-using product before it leaves the dealer's or a consignee's possession;[12]

- send a report to NRCan with information about an energy-using product before importing it or shipping it between provinces, if the product is not already listed in the NRCan database;

- send a report to NRCan about the modification or export of below-standard energy-using products that have been imported or shipped between provinces within 120 days of their import or shipment;

- provide sample models of a product to NRCan for testing ad inspection if required;

- keep records about energy-using products for six years, unless authorised by the Minister to do otherwise; and

- assist NRCan inspectors.

To determine whether dealers (manufacturers, importers, sellers and lessors) are complying with labelling and standards requirements, NRCan relies on the following monitoring mechanisms:

- *self-monitoring by dealers* — dealers are required to be sure that the energy-using products they handle meet energy-efficiency requirements by ensuring that an energy-efficiency verification mark is on the energy-using product before the product leaves the dealer's possession or, if the dealer has passed the product on to a consignee, before it leaves the possession of the consignee.

- *tip and complaints* — NRCan follows up on tips and complaints made by consumers, product and retail competitors, and consumer and environmental organisations concerning the accuracy of claims made by dealers about a product's energy efficiency.

---

12. The energy-efficiency verification mark indicates that a province or an accredited certification organisation has verified the energy performance of the product and that it meets energy-efficiency standards on an on going basis.

- *information from inspectors and other government officials (labels only)* — NRCan works with other agencies to verify the presence of EnerGuide labels by systematic spot checks and compliance reviews.

- *report verification (standards only)* — NRCan checks the reports on energy-using products that dealers are required to submit before the products are imported or shipped from one province to another.

- *independent product testing (standards only)* — in cases where enforcement action is being considered, NRCan arranges for the independent testing of products under the following priorities:

  - a product from a dealer with a history of non-compliance;

  - a product that performs neat minimum levels or close to best performance in its class;

  - a newly regulated product; and

  - a product that is not regulated in another jurisdiction.

The guide emphasises NRCan's focus on self-monitoring, reporting, voluntary compliance and collaboration, but explains enforcement measures that can be used if the labels and standards laws are violated. There are three principal enforcement actions. First, non-compliant products, or those without proper reporting documentation, can be denied entry through customs. Second, NRCan may negotiate remedial settlements with dealers who violate the laws. Among the remedial actions that could be negotiated are: recalling non-compliant products, notifying and/or compensating purchasers of noncompliant products, reviewing and modifying manufacturing processes and quality assurances procedures, and promoting energy efficiency in product advertising. Third, dealers who fail to comply with labelling and standards rules can be prosecuted, with fines up to CAD 200 000. Dealers who knowingly provide false or misleading information about a product, who tamper with EnerGuide labels, who fail to assist inspectors or who otherwise contravene the law can be fined up to CAD 10 000. Each day that offences continue are counted as a separate offence. In addition to issuing fines, the court may also order violators to stop activities that result in continuation of the offence, publish information about the offence, pay for the testing expenses related to the offence and post bonds to ensure future compliance.

Programme Evaluation

The principal role of programme evaluation is to maintain the credibility of labels and standards programmes in the eyes of policymakers and the public. Another purpose is to keep programme personnel accountable for their actions, and to provide early feedback on programme problems and opportunities. Programme evaluation (and performance measurement) helps support better decision-making in order to:

- improve the performance of the organisation with respect to economy, efficiency, effectiveness, service quality and financial diligence;[13]

- improve control measures for programme designers, managers and government ministers and accountability mechanisms for external reviewers such as auditors and legislators;

- inform the budgetary process by providing decision takers with information which links programme performance and budgets; and

- motivate staff to improve performance (OECD, 1994).

To fulfil these roles, measurement and evaluation efforts must focus on various stages of the policy and programme stream. It is

---

13. Economy — obtaining resources at lowest cost possible. Efficiency — the relationship between output and the resources used to produce them. Effectiveness — the extent to which the intended objectives or outcomes are achieved. Service quality — the relation between programme output and programme delivery encompassing timeliness, accessibility, accuracy and continuity of services, and the level of comfort and courtesy given to users. Financial diligence — revenue earning, user charging and grant dispensing organisations have objectives related timeliness and client burden.

important that four major programme elements be measured and evaluated — programme inputs, programme outputs, programme outcomes and market outcomes — in a coherent way (NRCan, 1996 and 1998). Each element, and the links between them, can give useful insights into how programmes can be improved. In the context of labels and standards,

■ *programme inputs* include the funds and personnel time required to develop, administer and evaluate the programmes (and the cost of any incentives offered in conjunction with targets),

■ *programme outputs* include the number of products for which labels and standards have been developed, and the ambitiousness of the energy savings and GHG emissions reductions sought,

■ *programme outcomes* include the changes in energy-efficiency distribution of products offered on the market, and changes in purchasing patterns,

■ *market outcomes* include the actual energy efficiency improvements and GHG emissions reductions beyond business as usual, as measured by the changing profile of new product sales and by performance of the products in actual use.

Programme evaluation, especially that focused on market outcomes, can be difficult in the best of circumstances. But it is harder and more costly still when policies and programmes are not designed from their inception to be evaluated. [14] To facilitate later evaluation, programmes should be designed with the following attributes:

■ *Clear Programme Goals*. Programmes should have explicit, and to the extent possible, measurable, goals against which performance can be measured.

---

14. *Additional discussion of the measurement and evaluation of energy efficiency policies and programmes can be found in IEA, 1996.*

- *Data Collection Co-ordination.* The data needed for programme evaluation is often similar to those required for programme implementation. From the outset of the programme, the data activities for both the implementation and evaluation phases should be co-ordinated in order to reduce the overall data collection and analysis effort.

- *Business as Usual (BAU) Baseline.* Programmes should be established against the background of a credible BAU baseline of energy use and GHG emissions with relevant corrections for business cycles, economic trends and technological change.

- *Integration of Planning and Evaluation.* Planning and evaluation are two closely related activities, which must inform each other. Planning involves setting targets that are realistic for a given level of policy ambition. Evaluation involves judging actual programme performance against those targets. The evaluation results must then be fed back into the planning system in the form of improved bases for planning future programmes and, perhaps, revising targets for the current programme.

- *Correlation with End-Use Indicators.* In-depth evaluations, though expensive, can ultimately save governments money by increasing programme performance and efficiency. Still, techniques for correlating evaluation results with less costly energy use indicators should be developed in order to achieve the same programme performance, efficiency and credibility benefits with fewer in-depth evaluations.

Certainly, the true market outcomes (the actual energy efficiency improvements, energy savings and GHG emissions reductions beyond what would have occurred in the absence of the programme) is the most important element to enumerate. However, direct measurement of the actual energy savings (with large scale in-field monitoring) resulting from labels and standards is difficult and expensive. In fact, given the nature of measuring energy savings (or absence of energy use) from a hypothetical business as usual (BAU) baseline, it is probably impossible to know with absolute certainty the true market outcomes of labels and standards, or for that matter of any other energy efficiency policy. The trick is to find a combination of measurements and supportable assumptions from which a low-cost, sufficiently-certain picture of market effects can be drawn.

The examples below describe recent evaluations of programme and market outcomes, and some research into techniques for increasing the reliability of assumptions.

Programme Outcomes — Implementation Compliance and Actor Impacts

The European Union's Directives on labelling (92/75/EEC) and minimum energy efficiency standards (96/57/EC) explicitly instruct the Commission to evaluate programmes carried out under these directives. Thus far, two complementary aspects of the programmes have been investigated: (1) implementation compliance and actor impacts and (2) appliance purchasing trends.

The first evaluation examined the extent of formal compliance with the labelling directives and the impact of the scheme on different actors (Winward, 1998) (Schiellerup, 1999). The evaluation was based mostly on survey methods, including:

- A survey of all EU Member State Governments and their agencies
- An inspection of shops in each of the Member States
- Interviews with senior managers in European appliance manufacturers
- Interviews with senior retail staff
- In-the-home interviews with consumers who had recently purchased a cold appliance
- In-the-street interviews with consumers who were in the process of shopping for a major appliance

■ Re-analysis of data generated by an independent test laboratory, to compare the findings with the performance claims made on the labels by the manufacturers of those appliances.

The compliance part of the examination was something of a cross between a conformity assessment exercise (in terms of its subject) and a programme evaluation (in terms of its focus on improving programme design, rather than judging individual actors). The basic criteria for assessing compliance are very clear — are the laws on the books? are appliances being labelled? are the labels accurate? are authorities making an effort to enforce the laws? are governments providing complementary information campaigns? The evaluation investigated these basic questions within the framework the responsibilities assigned to EU Member State governments, appliance suppliers (manufacturers) and appliance dealers by the law, namely:

■ *EU Member State governments* — Translating directives into Member State law, taking all necessary measures to ensure that all suppliers and dealers in their territory fulfil their obligations and ensuring that the labelling scheme is accompanied by educational and promotional information campaigns aimed at encouraging more responsible use of energy by private customers.

■ *Suppliers* — Providing the labels and fiches to the dealers, fulfilling their responsibility for the accuracy of the labels and fiches, and establishing and making available technical information sufficient to enable assessment of the accuracy of the labels and fiches.

■ *Dealers* — Placing the correct labels, in the appropriate language, on the outside of the appliance in such a way as to be clearly visible and not obscured, and providing the required information with mail order and other distance selling.

In terms of legal implementation, all 15 EU Member States have now implemented the cold appliance labelling directive (94/2/EC), but most were late in doing so. Only four countries met implementation deadline of January 1995, an additional seven countries completed the procedure within one year after the deadline, and the remaining four were staggered over the next three years. The last country implemented in October 1998.

As for supplier and dealer compliance, the evaluators found:

"The overall level of compliance is disappointing, both in terms of the number of appliances fully labelled in the shops and in terms of continuing controversy over the accuracy of the declared values on the labels. Independent testing was only able to confirm the energy efficiency class on the label for a little over a third of the appliances tested. Taken together, it is possible that as few as one in five machines in the shops, across all 15 EU Member States, are accurately and fully labelled."

As revisions to the implementing directive are not expected to take effect until 2001, there will need to be operational improvements within the context of the present law.

While the examination of compliance reveals what parts of the programme need improvement, the evaluation of the scheme's impact on different actors gives clues into how the deficiencies might be remedied. The interviews with consumers, manufacturers and retailers gives insights into the attitudes and concerns that play a large role in determining how well the labelling programme works in encouraging the purchases of more energy-efficient appliances. For example, based on queries into consumers' understanding and concern about appliance energy use, their concern about the environment and their awareness, comprehension and trust of the label suggest that "the two keys to improving the effectiveness (in terms of changing buying behaviour) of the labelling scheme are to increase the proportion of labelled appliances in the shops, and to persuade individual consumers that energy use is an important criterion in buying appliances." Interviews with manufacturers revealed that their attitudes towards the energy label as a policy tool were becoming more positive, but that the process of distributing labels still needs improvement, and there is uncertainty about the legal responsibilities of different parts of the supply and dealer chain. Manufacturers also claimed that market shares had not changed at the level of appliance manufacturers, but there had been shifts at the level component makers. Interview with retailers revealed the most negative attitudes towards the labelling scheme. Retailers believe the scheme is an unwelcome chore, both for themselves and the manufacturers, and that the distribution systems for labels does not recognise retailing constraints. Their actions and responses suggest that some of them have little understanding (or regard) for the obligations the directives place on them.

Lastly, the evaluators found need for improvement in testing procedures, test data distribution and non-compliance penalties.

Programme Outcomes — Purchasing Trends

The second EU evaluation examined the appliances purchasing trends associated with the cold appliance labelling programme (and the announced standards programme) using a database containing market and energy data for models sold during 1994-1996 in eleven of the most populous EU countries[15] (Waide, 1999a & 1999b). The database combined market data listing annual sales and price by model (purchased from market research companies) and technical data on each cold appliance offered for sale in the EU (gathered from several sources, but principally the European white goods manufacturers association CECED). Unique software was developed to resolve the numerous data quality issues encountered in matching the market and technical data for each model, and a correction methodology was used to compensate for biases arising from incomplete energy data series. Once the database was

---

15. The cold appliance labelling directive was issued in January 1994 (to take effect in January 1995); the standards directive was issued in September 1996 (to take effect in September 1999). Though the standards directive was issued late in the period of analysis, and implemented well after the period, it could conceivably have had some effect during the analysis period. The imminent development of the standards programme was widely known, and manufacturers could be expected to begin the process of bringing their product lines into compliance with the directive.

operational, it was possible to track the efficiency trends of models sold in each of the eleven countries, and to compare them with the pre-programme analysis done by the Group for Efficient Appliances (GEA, 1993). Though efforts are underway to repeat this type of thorough database analysis for 1997 and 1998, it is has been possible to anticipate the findings by surveying the cold appliances offered for sale on the German market at the Domotechnica trade fair at the beginning of 1999.

This market analysis found that the sales-weighted annual average energy-efficiency index fell 6.0% from 1990/92 to 1994, and an additional 4.5% from 1994 to 1996.[16] The movement towards greater sales shares for the higher energy label classes is shown in Figure 3.4.[17] The analysis also indicated that the efficiency profiles of national markets vary considerably, such that the 1996 sales-weighted energy efficiency index for Germany was 77.8, but for the United Kingdom was 101.7.

The analysis also revealed some interesting aspects about the European market in relation to the labelling programme.

For example, it was found the sub-tropical and tropical models were at least 7% more efficient than the average model in 1996. This suggests that "there is no market-based rationale to support the preferential treatment of sub-tropical and tropical class appliances as is currently embodied in the minimum energy performance standards Directive."

---

16. Recall that the EU energy efficiency index is defined as the annual energy consumption of the given appliance tested under standard conditions divided by a nominal EU average energy consumption for an appliance of the same type and storage volume characteristics. The market analysis found the EU cold appliance sales-weighted annual energy efficiency index to be: 102.2 (1990/92), 96.1 (1994), 93.9 (1995) and 91.8 (1996).

17. Analyses of the shifts in model efficiencies have been carried out in North America as well, for example see Figures 1-1, 1-2 and 1-3

Figure 3.4 EU Cold Appliance Sales Share by Energy Label Class for 1994 to 1996 (also showing the distribution of GEA models by label class)

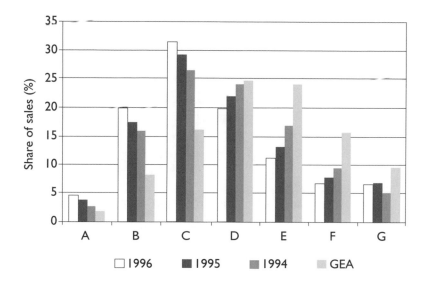

Source: Waide, 1999b.

The analysis also revealed two market characteristics that might be thought of as "programme signatures." These particularities in the market profiles suggest the direct influence of the labels and standards programmes. The labelling signature was the development of peaks in the number of models (as well as sales of products) with energy efficiency indices just slightly into the next better efficiency categories during 1994-96 (Figure 3.5). The model peaks suggest that manufacturers preferentially positioned products to just pass the threshold into a higher energy class. The sales peaks suggest the interest of consumers in products in the higher categories, or perhaps the selective promotion of these particular products.

Figure 3.5 Comparison of the Sales-Weighted and Model-Weighted Distribution of all EU Cold Appliances by Efficiency Index in 1996

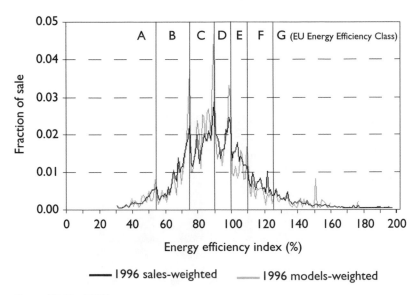

Source: Waide, 1999b.

The standards signature was revealed at the Domotechnica trade show in the range of appliances offered for sale in Germany. The fact that products in classes D, E, F and G accounted for only 7.5% of the models offered, indicates that manufacturers had already phased out appliances that would be prohibited from sale beginning in September 1999.

In conclusion, the market analysis evaluation found:

"It is necessarily speculative to imagine how the energy efficiency of the European cold appliance market would have progressed without the stimulus provided by the two European Directives; however, the average market efficiency had been static or had even shown a slight deterioration in the years immediately preceding the two Directives. Furthermore, from the development of tell tale characteristics (programme signatures) in the product offer energy efficiency distribution it seems certain that the two Directives have had an appreciable impact on the market and most likely that the majority of the measured efficiency improvements are attributable to their influence."

Estimating Market Outcomes

Assessing the market outcomes, i.e., energy savings, induced by labels and standards is methodologically and practically difficult. Energy savings are impossible to measure directly. They can only be observed as the difference between two energy use measurements (Meier, 1997). Theoretically, the best two measurements to compare would be: (1) the energy used in actual operating situations by all products covered by labels and standards, and (2) the energy used in actual operating situations by these same products had the labels and standards not been implemented. The latter case, however, is purely hypothetical and unmeasurable, since labels and standards influence entire markets and are not amenable to the use of statistical control groups. This, along with the need to use sampling methods to keep measuring costs low, makes it necessary to *estimate*, rather than measure, programme energy savings.

Good data provide the foundation for good energy savings estimates. The relevant data and their relationships to one another are illustrated in the schematic in Figure 3.6. The columns show the various types of energy use data that might be collected — product-specific data as reported on labels or certification documents (column r), taken from independent laboratory tests (column I), and gathered from field measurements or submetered utility records (column f), and household billing data (column b).[18] For some products, the data from labels, certification documents and

---

18. *Laboratory measurements are particularly useful in evaluation programmes. They are instrumental in compliance monitoring. Furthermore, if calibrated correctly, they are faster and less expensive alternatives to field measurements in market outcome evaluations.*

laboratory tests are fundamentally different from those obtained by field measurements. Some tests have energy use as their metric, but others have Coefficients of Performance (COP) or Energy Efficiency Ratio (EER) data. Meaningful comparison of COP or EER data and measured energy use data requires information on climatic, behavioural and other factors. The rows in Figure 3.6 show the product coverage — product purchases or stocks with (row **P**), without (row **N**) and before (row **B**) the labelling and standards programmes.[19] The "Non-existent programme" row (**N**) is hypothetical. Secondarily, the rows show whether the data are for the entire appliance population (rows *g*) or for samples thereof (rows *s*).

The heavily shaded cells **P***fg* and **N***fg* — the field measured data of the product energy use with and without the labelling and standards programmes — represent the theoretical best values to be estimated. The lightly shaded cells represent the types of data that might be conceivably obtained. In some cases, though, the costs for the extensive data may be high. For purposes of orientation, the data collected in the EU evaluations mentioned in the previous two sections are labelled. The EU purchasing trends evaluation described in the previous section examined the relationship between **P***rg* and **B***rg* (the reported energy use of the product purchases or stocks before and after the labelling and standards programmes were implemented). And the EU compliance evaluation examined the relationship between **P***rs* and **P***ls* — energy use values as reported and as measured in laboratory tests — to detect reporting errors.

---

19. *To maximise the usefulness, and minimise the cost, of data collection activities, steps should be taken to integrate the data collected as part of the analysis during the programme development phase with those used in the evaluation scheme.*

Figure 3.6 Schematic of Data Issues Associated With Measuring Market Outcomes

Purchases or Stocks	Product Test Data energy use metric (kWh/a, kWh/cycle, ...) or energy efficiency metric (COP, EER, ...)*		Product Energy Use Data	Household or Establishment Energy Use Data
	reported on labels or certification documents. (r)	laboratory measured (l)	field measured (or submetered billing) (f)	billing records (b)
Programme (P)				
global population (g)	Prg		Pfg	
sample population (s)	Prs	Pls	Pfs	
Nonexistent programme — hypothetical (N)				
global population (g)			Nfg	
sample population (s)				
Before programme (B)				
global population (g)	Brg			
sample population (s)			Bfs	

* COP = Coefficients of Performance (COP); EER = Energy Efficiency Ratios
Source: IEA

The relationships between the various columns and rows are very important in assessing the changes brought about by labels and standards.

Comparing rows **B** and **P**, before and after labels and standards implementation, encompasses the changes in product technologies and shifts in consumers' purchasing patterns that occurred concurrently with the programmes. Of course, some of the changes are caused by the programmes, while others are merely coincidental. Expert analysis of the **B** and **P** data in the context of overall market and consumer trends give clues to which of the technologies and purchasing patterns would have occurred in the absence of labelling and standards programmes.

Sometimes, the difference between rows **B** and **P** is taken to be an upper limit to the effects of programmes. The logic is that energy savings attributable to programmes cannot possibly be greater than the actual difference between before and after. This is true in many cases, but not necessarily all. For example, it is conceivable that some new products with labels and standards programmes could use more energy than the products they replace. In this case, there would appear to be no energy savings, but instead there energy growth. The actual energy savings due to the programmes are greater than those suggested by the before and after data alone.

There are two other important issues that complicate the comparison of rows **B** and **P**, especially at the level of field measurements and billing records — product degradation and changes in consumer behaviour. Product degradation issues arise when old (used) products are compared with new ones. The difference in energy use between a new product and a 15 year-old one that it replaces is due not only to differences in technology (whether or not related to labels and standards), but also performance degradation occurring with age and insufficient maintenance. The other issue concerns whether consumers are changing they way they use their products, and if the labels and standards are influencing that behaviour in any way. The classic example, is the much-debated rebound effect. It is important to know, for example, whether consumers heat their homes to different comfort levels depending on whether they purchase a less efficient furnace or a more efficient one? Or do they drive differently if they purchase a less efficient automobile or a more efficient one. Are the differences in costs, for example, sufficient to change consumers' behaviour.

The relationship between columns *r* and *l*, the reported and laboratory test values, concerns not only the manufacturers' commitment to truthful representation of their products, but also the quality of the test procedures in yielding replicable results.

The relationships between columns l, f and b, the laboratory tested, field-measured and billing data, concern the ability of the tests to estimate energy use in real world situations of varying climatic and behavioural conditions. "Realism of testing conditions is typically sacrificed in order to achieve simplicity and repeatability" (Meier, 1997a). Nonetheless, it is important to recalibrate tests to real operating conditions periodically as products and their features evolve, and different factors determine field energy use and observed savings.

Data collection especially in laboratories and field measurement is expensive, so samples are frequently used. The relationship between row s and g, sampling and global data, concern issues of representativeness and scale-up. That is, do the samples adequately represent the entire product range and range of operating conditions? and how are conclusions drawn from a particular sample generalised to the more global population of products and conditions.

Data in the lightly shaded areas of Figure 3.6 have been collected and analysed in numerous studies, but in no instance have all the data types been collected in a co-ordinated way to enable systematic estimation of the real market outcomes of labels and standards programmes. Nonetheless, the various ad hoc studies have revealed some interesting facets of product-efficiency programmes. A recent survey of various testing studies found (Meier, 1997a).

■ "The impact of efficiency standards on refrigerator energy use is the best documented. Most verifications fall into two categories: (1) field verification of laboratory tests [comparing columns l and f] or (2) observation of energy savings from replacement with more efficient units [a special type of comparison of $\mathbf{B}fs$ and $\mathbf{P}fs$]. In both cases, savings estimates are based on the difference between the new and old units. There is usually no attempt to adjust the savings to reflect what might have happened without standards, which sometimes leads to an overestimate of the savings resulting from standards."

■ In the United States comparisons of labelled, laboratory-tested and field-measured energy use of refrigerators found wide variations between the values for particular units, but *on average* the labelled and laboratory-tested values were very similar to the observed field measured values. "This information makes it possible to confidently predict field energy use of new refrigerators and savings likely to occur from higher efficiency models" (Meier, 1997a). In Sweden, field measurements were found to be 46% less than labelled values (based on ISO test procedures) for refrigerators and 17% less for freezers. In Japan, actual consumption of refrigerators was found to be much higher than the laboratory tests (using JIS test procedures) — from 20% higher in the winter to 140% higher in the summer. These discrepancies were reduced in 1995 when Japan switched to the ISO test procedures, raising test measurement results by 40-50%.

■ Studies in the US have shown that refrigerators represent such a large part of total house electricity consumption, and the savings associated with the purchase of new, standards-compliant models so consistent, that energy savings are readily observed in lower utility bills. The observed reduction in utility bills corresponded reasonably well to the expected savings.

■ The savings resulting from efficiency standards are difficult to observe for heating and cooling equipment because actual consumption is influenced (at least more so than with refrigerators) by variations in occupant behaviour and weather. "Laboratory-measured differences in efficiency generally give accurate estimates of percentage savings, but give poor estimates of absolute savings." The reasons is that most laboratory tests for heating and cooling equipment measure only efficiency or Coefficient of Performance (COP) rather than energy consumption. An additional engineering calculation, requiring information on the distribution system, the buildings thermal characteristics and the climate and the occupants' thermostat settings, is needed to convert COP to energy consumption. Finally, most laboratory tests measure steady-state efficiency rather than seasonal efficiency (which includes variations in efficiency resulting from part-load operation and other factors).

■ "Appliance efficiency standards are designed to reduce energy use and save consumers money. However, surprisingly little effort has been directed toward verifying that the costs of energy-related services have indeed occurred." Some studies have demonstrated impacts on utility bills. "There are frequent disputes about the actual incremental costs [of the products concerned]. ... For the first generation of appliance standards, the uncertainty in incremental cost is probably not so important because the payback times are still short. In subsequent generations, the incremental costs may deserve more careful attention" (Meier, 1997a).

As mentioned earlier there has been no systemic effort to collect and link all these types of data to estimate the energy savings from labels and standards. In the programme design stage, programme designers and political authorities, need to decide what level of evidence is adequate to show whether or not the programmes are having the desired effects, and design the sampling, testing and analysis to meet that level of desired confidence in the results. There must be an understood balance between the costs of conducting the tests and the confidence in programme performance desired. In his survey, Meier suggests that "(1) one can estimate the baseline and measure actual use with the programme, or (2) measure the difference in energy use between an old appliance and its efficient replacement. Neither approach is perfectly satisfying, but when both approaches demonstrate energy savings, as is the case on numerous occasions for many appliances, then the results are persuasive."

ASSESSMENTS OF ACTUAL AND EXPECTED RESULTS OF LABELS AND STANDARDS IN IEA COUNTRIES

A number of studies on country or regional levels have examined the benefits and costs of implementing labels and standards. Most of the studies have focused on *expected* (ex-ante) energy savings, CO_2 reductions and costs. A few have examined the *actual* (ex-post) results of the programmes. The results of several studies performed in Australia, Canada, the European Union, Switzerland and the United States are presented below.

AUSTRALIA

Actual Results

It is estimated that had the States not introduced the labels in 1986, the annual energy consumption of all new appliances of the labelled types sold in 1992 would have been about 11 per cent higher than it was, and total household electricity consumption would have been about 1.6 per cent higher (Wilkenfeld 1993). This represented a saving of about 630 GWh and about 0.65 Mt CO2 in 1992. The sales-weighted electricity consumption of refrigerators and freezers was estimated to be 12% below what it would have been without labelling, for dish washers 16% below, for clothes dryers 1% below and for air conditioners 6% below (Wilkenfeld, 1997).

Another study examined the labelling programme by comparing the present pattern of appliance purchases with what the pattern would be if all buyers had used the energy label plus the sales price to select the model with the lowest life cycle. That is if all buyers were perfectly informed rational and perfectly informed. The conclusion were that, for refrigerators purchased in 1992, the energy savings were about 35% of what they would have been if all buyers had chosen the mode cost-effective model in the size and configuration they bought. The labels were achieving a third of theoretical potential. The figures were similar for dishwashers (36%) and air conditioners (39%), and substantial less for clothes dryers (13%) (Wilkenfeld, 1997).

Expected Results

George Wilkenfeld and Associates conducted numerous studies of household appliances in the 1990s to provide a basis for various proposed efficiency labels and standards programmes. The analysis has recently been be rerun to estimate the impacts of the National Appliance and Equipment Energy Efficiency Program (NAEEEP) on national greenhouse gas emissions in the period 2000 to 2015 (AGO, 2000). The average impact of the all proposed NAEEEP programmes on household appliances, commercial air conditioners, commercial refrigeration, lighting, electric motors and industrial equipment is estimated to be about 7.2 Mt CO2-equivalent per year below business-as-usual over the during the Kyoto Protocol Commitment period 2008 to 2012. Most of the programmes, however, have not been implemented yet. The two that are already running, the appliance labelling programme and the refrigerator and water heater standards, are expected to reduce CO^2 emissions by approximately 0.38 Mt and 0.83 Mt per year in 2010. It is expected, though, that these programmes will be superseded by more ambitious programmes in the next several years.

CANADA

Actual Results

Canada's Energy Efficiency Regulations apply to equipment that uses 73 per cent of total residential energy. This ranges from almost all of the energy consumed in water heating to 72 per cent of energy used in heating, ventilation and air conditioning (HVAC) to 46 per cent of the energy used to operate appliances and lighting (NRCan, 2000).

NRCan has found the Regulations to have significantly affected the energy efficiency of new appliance models. The agency cites declines in energy use of 21 per cent for clothes washers and dryers, and between 29 and 38 per cent for refrigerators, freezers and dishwashers (Figure 4.1).

Figure 4.1 Average Energy Consumption of New Appliances, 1990 and 1997

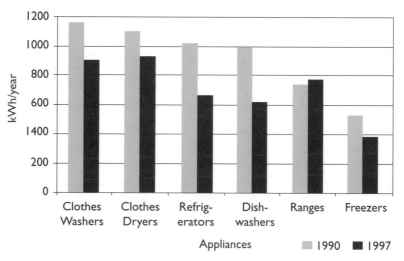

Source: NRCan, 2000.

Regulations, along with the EnerGuide labels, helped shift refrigerator sales towards more efficient models. Between 1990 and 1997, the sales-weighted average consumption of new refrigerators decreased by 37.6 percent, from 61.7 kWh per cubic foot in 1990 to 38.6 kWh per cubic foot in 1997 (Figure 4.2). The energy efficiency of top-mount refrigerators has improved 32 per cent since 1990, despite a 7 per cent increase in the size of these appliances (Figure 4.3).

Regulations have also greatly influenced the average efficiency of natural gas furnaces. Normal low-efficiency natural gas furnaces have disappeared from the market since 1990.

Figure 4.2 Distribution of Refrigerator Sales According to Energy Consumption, 1990 and 1997

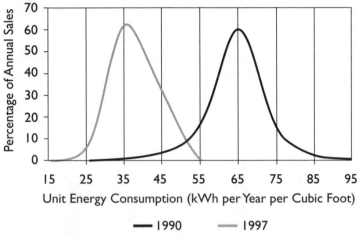

Source: NRCan, 2000.

Figure 4.3 Size and Energy Consumption of New Type 3 Refrigerators, 1991 and 1998

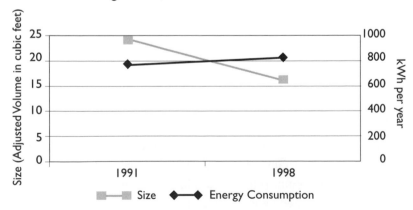

Source: NRCan, 2000.

Figure 4.4 Energy Use Trends for Refrigerators, 1991 and 1998

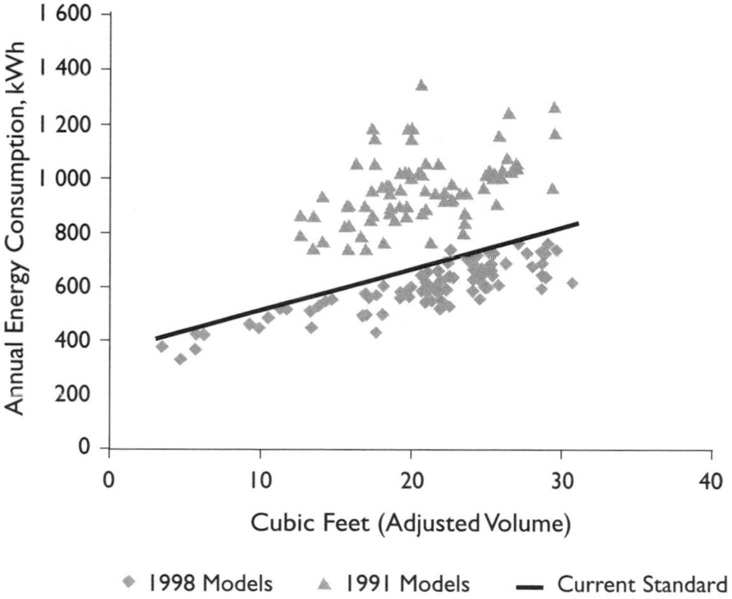

◆ 1998 Models   ▲ 1991 Models   ── Current Standard

Source: NRCan, 2000.

Expected Results

In February 1995, NRCan established energy performance levels for the following products, which account for about 65 per cent of residential energy demand:

■ major residential appliances — electric clothes dryers; clothes washers; integrated stacking washer-dryers; dishwashers; refrigerators, freezers and combination refrigerator-freezers; and electric and gas ranges;

■ space-conditioning equipment — room air conditioners; single-package and split-system air conditioners and heat pumps; ground- or water-source and internal water-loop heat pumps; and gas furnaces;

■ water-heating equipment — oil-fired, gas-fired and electric;

■ lighting equipment — fluorescent and incandescent reflector lamps; and

■ other energy-using equipment — fluorescent lamp ballasts and electric motors.

NRCan estimates that this first set of energy efficiency regulations will produce aggregate energy savings of 40 petajoules in the 2000, increasing to more than 120 petajoules by 2020 (Table 4.1). The shares of the projected energy savings by 2020 are approximately 57% natural gas, 40% electricity and 2% electricity (NRCan, 1996). The energy savings in 2020 are equivalent to the average annual space-heating requirements of 1.5 million houses in Canada. An earlier study estimated the net consumer benefits per appliance (over the life, discounted at 7% real) are estimated at CAD 34 for refrigerator, CAD 42 per freezer, and CAD 918 per natural gas furnace (EMR, 1994).

Table 4.1   Summary of Estimated Residential Energy Savings (petajoules)

	1995	2000	2005	2010	2015	2020
Natural Gas	5.46	22.86	46.61	66.29	69.99	73.69
Electricity	5.25	17.99	31.28	44.09	49.33	51.76
Oil	0.21	0.90	1.80	2.61	2.75	2.89
Total	10.92	41.75	79.69	112.99	122.07	128.34

Source: NRCan, 1996

EUROPEAN UNION

Actual Results

The evaluation of the market outcomes of the E.U. labelling programme (described in Chapter 3) found that the sales-weighted annual average energy efficiency of refrigerators and freezers improved 6.0% from 1990/92 to 1994, and an additional 4.5% from 1994 to 1996. The analysis also indicated that the efficiency profiles of national markets vary considerably, such that the 1996 sales-weighted energy-efficiency index for Germany was 77.8, but for the United Kingdom was 101.7 (Waide, 1999b).

Expected Results

The same assessment found that the cumulative energy consumption of refrigerators and freezers sold in Europe between 1991 and 2000 is likely to be 16 % lower than otherwise had been the case and 21% lower by 2020 (some 212 and 528 TWh respectively) as a result of the E.U. labelling and standards programmes. The annual energy savings are forecast to reach 8.5 TWh/year by 2000, 26 TWh/year by 2010 and 35 TWh/year by 2020. This last figure is equivalent to an annual saving in electricity demand of 1.7% of all electricity consumption in the EU in 1995. Annual CO_2 savings are forecast to reach 4.2 Megatonnes (Mt) per year by 2000, 12.6 Mt/year by 2010 and 17.2 Mt/year by 2020. Cumulative CO_2 savings of 104 Mt are forecast for 2010 (Waide, 1999b).

The savings estimates are based on the assumptions that *without* labels and standards the efficiency of refrigerators and freezers would have been frozen at 1991 levels, and that *with* labels and standards the efficiency ceases to improve after 1999. The pessimistic assumptions underlying each of the two cases counterbalance each other, to a certain extent, in the calculation of expected savings.

At an E.U. average electricity price of 0.13 EUR/kWh, these efficiency improvements will reduce the running costs of each refrigerator or freezer by about 275 EUR over a typical 15 year lifetime. With an E.U. average of about 1.8 refrigerators and freezers per household, the reduction in the typical household's electricity bill will amount to approximately 33 EUR per household per year or 495 EUR over the appliances' lifetimes. At the level of the European Union, the customer energy bill savings are expected to be worth 4.6 billion EUR per year by 2020. Given that the average B class refrigerator or freezer was 73 EUR (or 18%) more expensive than an average E class cold appliance sold in Europe in 1996, but used 143 kWh/year (18.6 EUR) less electricity, then the simple payback period associated with buying an appliance having an energy efficiency index of 70% as opposed to 102% was 3.9 years. This payback is expected to improve in coming years as the cost of a class B appliance compared to an equivalent E appliance is likely to diminish as class B becomes the norm (Waide, 1999b).

SWITZERLAND

Actual Results

The results of the Swiss Target Value programme are shown in Table 4.2. Though none of the product categories achieved their targets by the end of 1997, substantial progress was made for some product categories.

Table 4.2   Results of Swiss Target Value Programme, as of the end of 1997

Equipment	Deadline	Percentage of equipment attaining target value by end of 1997
Refrigerators (*** or fewer)	1996	69
Refrigerators (****)	1996	87
Freezers upright	1996	86
Freezers chest	1996	53
Photocopiers	1997	88

Printers	1997	0
Ovens	1998	71
Dishwashers	1998	88
Dryers	1998	70
Clothes Washers	1998	82
Fax Machines	1998	24
Televisions	1998	43
Video Cassette Recorders	1999	9
Monitors	2000	5
Personal Computers	2000	13

Source: SFOE, 1999

UNITED STATES

Actual Results

Market surveys in the United States have shown evidence of the
effects of standards. Figure 4.5 shows the efficiencies of the top-
mount refrigerators offered on the market in 1989 (prior to the first
Federal standards) and 1993 (after revised standards were
implemented), along with the maximum energy use allowed the 1990
and 1993 standards. Many 1989 models already met the 1990
standard, but many others were forced off the market by the
standards. An entire new generation of models had to be developed
to meet the 1993 standards (Geller, 1997). Figure 4.6 shows the
trends in sales-weighted average energy use of refrigerators in the
United States. It shows that refrigerators were steadily getting bigger
and more energy consuming until the first oil shock and California's
introduction of standards in 1976 (becoming effective in 1978). With
the subsequent California and Federal standards, average refrigerator
energy use has declined to a less than a third of the 1974 level.

Figure 4.5 Efficiency Gains with Standards in the United States (for top-mount auto-defrost refrigerators)

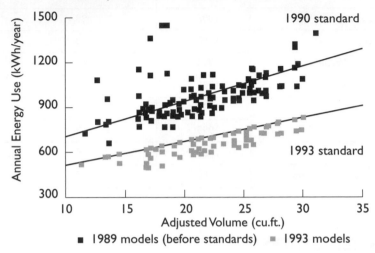

■ 1989 models (before standards) ▦ 1993 models

Source: LBNL, 1995

Figure 4.6 Energy Use of New Refrigerators in the United States

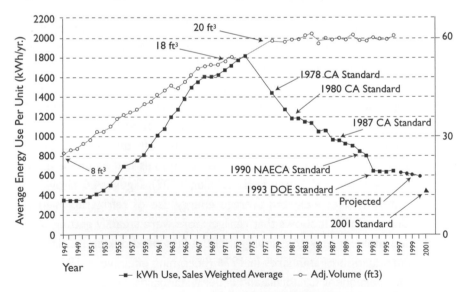

The right vertical (macro) scale shows the number of 1-GW baseload powerplants (running 500 hours/year) required to serve 150 million refrigerators and freezers.

Source: Geller-Goldstein Szilaar Lecture, 1999.

One retrospective study examined the price, amenity and equity effects of the 1990 and 1993 U.S. refrigerator standards on consumers (Greening, 1996). More precisely, it evaluated the effects on real refrigerator prices, refrigerator volumes and features, and low income households. The analysis of national refrigerator sales data showed that following the introduction of the standards: (1) real prices did not increase, and in some case decreased, and (2) refrigerator features, such as size and amenities, were not diminished. Average real prices for units meeting the 1990 standards remained unchanged from earlier models, and units meeting 1993 standards were 14% less expensive than previous models. Food and freezer volumes were relatively stable up until the 1993 standard, and decreased afterwards. Normalised to food and freezer volumes, the net reduction in real refrigerator prices declined 8% during 1987 to 1993.[20] Though the time series data were limited, the analysis found that the standards did not appear to have disrupted the historical decline in refrigerator prices. The authors postulated that while it is possible that the standards may have dampened the historical trend in price reduction for particular product classes, if it occurred it was probably the result of increased amenities rather than the cost of energy efficiency features. The authors caution that their results do not imply that manufacturers did not incur costs in meeting the standards, but that the costs were not passed on to consumers in the form of higher prices. As for equity issues, the analysis of refrigerator ownership data in California showed that lower income households were just as likely to have high efficiency units as higher income levels.

Expected Results

A 1998 LBNL study of the potential energy, monetary and carbon impacts of appliances and equipment standards aimed at U.S. residential sector found:

---

20. For all refrigerators sold, average electricity consumption decreased 15% for units meeting the 1990 standards, and an additional 34% for united meeting the 1993 standards, a net decrease of 44%.

"Energy savings (beyond those resulting from improvements in efficiency likely to occur anyway) from the standards to be substantial. Standards for the appliances analysed[21] are expected to save a total of 10.6 exajoules (EJ) of primary energy between 1990 and 2010. (Table 4.3) About 57% of this savings is electricity, 41.4% natural gas, and only 1.5% distillate oil. Annual energy savings will increase as energy efficient appliances replace the existing stock, peaking in 2004 at 0.69 EJ. These savings represent more than 3% of the projected residential energy consumption in 2004.. Projected carbon reductions are approximately 9 Mt of carbon per year from 2000 through 2010, an amount roughly equal to 4% of U.S. residential carbon emissions in 1990 (Koomey, 1998)".

The assessment used historical and projected shipments of equipment, a detailed stock accounting model, measured and estimated unit energy savings associated with the standards, estimated incremental capital costs, demographic data, and fuel price data at the finest level of geographic disaggregation available. It explicitly account for improvements in efficiency likely to occur in the absence of standards.

The largest cumulative savings for the analysis period come from the standard on showerheads, which saves roughly 2.2 EJ of electric, gas, and oil water heating energy from 1994 to 2010. This result is primarily due to their long lifetimes (20 years), the large decrease in unit energy consumption due to the 1994 standards, and very slow progress in the baseline efficiency. Following close behind is the gas water heater standard, which saves a total of 2 EJ through 2010. The 1993 refrigerator standard saves 1.35 EJ of primary energy during the period, while the other standards individually each save less than 1 EJ.

---

21. The study included standards on central and room heating equipment, air conditioners, water heaters, refrigerator/freezers, freezers, ranges and ovens, dishwashers, clothes washers, dryers, swimming pool heaters, showers, and faucets. It excluded standards on refrigerator/freezers and freezers due in 2001 and room air conditioners due in 2000, as well as standards on fluorescent lamps and ballasts, incandescent reflectors and motors, which are applicable to all sectors.

According to the study, efficiency standards in the residential sector have been a highly cost-effective policy instrument for promoting energy efficiency. For consumers, the standards are expected to add $13 billion to the cost of appliances, but save $46 billion in energy consumption between 1990 and 2010. The Federal government's programme expenditures have been $200 million. Thus, $165 of consumer savings are expected for each dollar spent by the Federal government. Benefit/cost ratios for specific end-uses range from just below 1.0 for the least cost-effective standard (natural gas dryers) to more than 100 for the most cost effective standard (natural gas room heating) (Koomey, 1998).

Table 4.3   Summary of National Effects of U.S. Residential
Efficiency Standards in 2010

End-use	Fuel	Annual in 2010				
		Primary Energy Savings (PJ)	Savings (Mt-C)	Bill Savings (M 1995 USD/yr)	Incremental Costs (M 1995 USD/yr)	Net Benefit (M 1995 USD/yr)
Central Air Conditioner	Electricity	00	0	00	00	00
Clothes Washer	Electricity	52	0.75	390	05	385
Clothes Dryer	Electricity	51	0.74	397	235	163
Dishwasher	Electricity	25	0.35	186	55	131
Dishwasher Motors	Electricity	20	0.28	150	62	88
Freezer 1990	Electricity	01	0.02	09	02	07
Freezer 1993	Electricity	06	0.08	42	26	16
Faucets	Electricity	19	0.27	153	25	128
Heat Pumps	Electricity	00	0	01	00	00
Refrigerators 1990	Electricity	05	0.07	39	15	24
Refrigerators 1993	Electricity	69	0.94	542	247	295
Room Air Conditioners	Electricity	01	0.02	12	01	10
Showers	Electricity	120	1.65	943	99	843
Water Heaters	Electricity	06	0.08	43	08	36
Central Heat	Natural Gas	05	0.07	28	08	19
Clothes Washer	Natural Gas	31	0.42	181	07	174
Clothes Dryer	Natural Gas	10	0.14	59	60	– 01
Dishwasher	Natural Gas	15	0.20	86	79	07

Cumulative 1990-2010						
Primary Energy Savings (PJ)	Savings (Mt-C)	Bill Savings (M 1995 USD/yr)	Incremental Costs (M 1995 USD/yr)	Net PV Benefit (M 1995 USD/yr)	Fuel	End-use
112	1.70	536	379	157	Electricity	Central Air Conditioner
721	10.37	3 239	40	3 198	Electricity	Clothes Washer
500	7.19	2 148	1 291	857	Electricity	Clothes Dryer
283	4.00	1 238	360	878	Electricity	Dishwasher
228	3.22	998	407	592	Electricity	Dishwasher Motors
39	0.58	213	55	158	Electricity	Freezer 1990
106	1.57	541	338	203	Electricity	Freezer 1993
207	2.85	894	152	743	Electricity	Faucet
46	0.67	262	129	133	Electricity	Heat Pump
220	3.01	1 228	507	720	Electricity	Refrigerators 1990
1 348	18.57	6 780	3 229	3 551	Electricity	Refrigerators 1993
214	3.12	1 147	123	1 024	Electricity	Room Air Conditioners
1 278	17.62	5 529	606	4 922	Electricity	Showers
724	10.32	4 186	740	3 446	Electricity	Water Heaters
132	1.81	532	158	374	Natural Gas	Central Heat
427	5.85	1 459	59	1 400	Natural Gas	Clothes Washer
100	1.38	330	340	– 10	Natural Gas	Clothes Dryer
169	2.32	564	524	40	Natural Gas	Dishwasher

		Annual in 2010				
End-use	Fuel	Primary Energy Savings (PJ)	Savings (Mt-C)	Bill Savings (M 1995 USD/yr)	Incremental Costs (M 1995 USD/yr)	Net Benefit (M 1995 USD/yr)
Faucets	Natural Gas	12	0.16	73	38	35
Ovens	Natural Gas	18	0.25	111	57	54
Room Heat	Natural Gas	00	0	00	00	00
Range	Natural Gas	27	0.37	163	65	98
Showers	Natural Gas	74	1.02	451	151	299
Water Heaters	Natural Gas	42	0.58	250	45	205
Central Heat	Distillate Oil	00	0	00	00	00
Clothes Washer	Distillate Oil	02	0.04	15	00	15
Dishwasher	Distillate Oil	01	0.02	07	06	02
Faucets	Distillate Oil	01	0.02	07	04	04
Showers	Distillate Oil	07	0.13	45	14	31
Water Heaters	Distillate Oil	01	0.01	04	01	03
Total	Electricity	374	5.24	2 906	780	2 125
Total	Natural Gas	234	3.21	1 402	511	891
Total	Distillate Oil	12	0.23	79	25	54
Total	All	620	8.68	4 387	1 316	3 071

Electricity expressed as primary energy at 3.165 kWh.primary/kWh.electricity
Cumulative carbon emissions calculated using electricity emissions factor for 2010. The error introduced is small because emission factors change little over the analysis period. Incremental costs based on annualised method. Cumulative costs and benefits present valued to 1995 at a 7% real discount rate.
Source: Koomey, 1998

Cumulative 1990-2010						
Primary Energy Savings (PJ)	Savings (Mt-C)	Bill Savings (M 1995 USD/yr)	Incremental Costs (M 1995 USD/yr)	Net PV Benefit (M 1995 USD/yr)	Fuel	End-use
128	1.76	415	227	188	Natural Gas	Faucets
237	3.25	840	454	386	Natural Gas	Ovens
19	0.25	92	01	91	Natural Gas	Room Heat
350	4.80	1 243	523	720	Natural Gas	Range
792	10.86	2 566	908	1 658	Natural Gas	Showers
2 014	27.62	8 268	1 512	6 756	Natural Gas	Water Heaters
00	0.00	00	00	00	Distillate Oil	Central Heat
31	0.59	123	04	118	Distillate Oil	Clothes Washer
12	0.23	47	38	09	Distillate Oil	Dishwasher
12	0.23	45	21	23	Distillate Oil	Faucets
75	1.42	276	85	191	Distillate Oil	Showers
25	0.47	117	19	99	Distillate Oil	Water Heaters
6 026	84.80	28 938	8 355	20 583	Electricity	Total
4 368	59.90	16 309	4 705	11 603	Natural Gas	Total
156	3.00	609	168	441	Distillate Oil	Total
10 550	147.70	45 856	13 229	32 627	All	Total

ISSUES FOR THE FUTURE

This chapter presents two issues that will need attention by the international community in the near future. The first involves technological changes — increased use of sensors and microcontrollers — in appliances and equipment that will make the development of simple and representative energy test protocols more difficult. The second involves the potential economies in programme development available from international programme collaboration. This will become more and more important in light of the increasing product globalisation and mounting interest by developing countries in product labels and standards as means of meeting energy and environmental objectives.

TESTING PROTOCOLS AND MICROCONTROLLERS[22]

Microcontrollers in combination with sensors are becoming commonplace in appliances and equipment of all sorts. Their ability to collect information, process it and decide how to operate enables appliances and equipment to match their operating characteristics better with their operating environments. For example, a dishwasher that can sense the degree of dirtiness of plates (through the optical properties of the wash water) can vary its wash cycle accordingly. Microcontrollers can be an effective tool to save energy, and will probably contribute more to saving energy in appliances and equipment in the next decade than will mechanical improvements (Meier, 1998).

Microcontrollers modify the operations of appliances and equipment in many different ways. Situations vary, but the energy savings come principally from five operating modifications:

---

22. This section draws heavily from Meier, 1998.

- skipping unneeded operations;
- adjusting output to actual requirements;
- performing services on demand;
- anticipating requirements by learning from previous cycles;
- reconciling conflicting requirements (through use of fuzzy logic and neural networks).

According to Meier, any one of these modifications can often reduce an appliance's energy use by 25%, combinations can yield savings as high as 75%.

These new control technologies present two major challenges to energy test protocols. First, they can be used to circumvent labels and standards, by being programmed to operate appliances and equipment with uncharacteristically low energy use while they are undergoing standard tests.[23] Second, existing test procedures can discourage the introduction of legitimate, energy-saving technologies that rely on microcontroller technology.

An example of the first case occurs with refrigerators. In Japan most refrigerators are now equipped with sophisticated microcontrollers, which are capable of, among other things, recognising when the refrigerator is undergoing an energy test. When the test conditions are sensed, the microcontroller modifies operations in ways that reduce energy consumption, such as switching off auxiliary fans or shortening the defrost cycle. Some manufacturers have achieved over 25% reductions in tested energy use without significant changes in the units' mechanical features, such as thickness of insulation and compressor efficiency. When operated in kitchens,

---

23. Several cases in the related realm of emissions testing of automobiles have resulted in criminal prosecution in the United States. One case involved General Motors, which programmed emissions control circuits in certain Cadillacs to go "open loop" (shut down) the speed exceeded 60 miles per hour or when the air conditioner was switched on. This gave the cars better acceleration. Neither of these very common operating conditions was part of the Federal emissions test. The U.S. EPA fined Cadillac $46 million and subsequently rewrote the regulations to prohibit all open loop operation (Cushman, 1995 and Meier, 1998).

these units use about the same amount of energy as older units not equipped with microcontrollers.

There are cases to the contrary, however, where real day-to-day energy savings resulting from microcontrollers are undetected by the test procedures. Such energy-saving modifications include:

■ variable-interval "adaptive" defrost in refrigerators;

■ variable-speed motors in air conditioners, heat pumps, and refrigerators;

■ soil sensors in dishwashers and clothes washers;

■ moisture and temperature sensors in clothes dryers;

■ replaceable control chips for appliances.

The problem is that the energy tests are based on almost entirely on mechanical performance characteristics and do not give proper credit for microcontroller-based operating characteristics. Thus energy labels and standards provide no incentive for manufacturers to incorporate such energy-savings innovations in their products.

Discrepancies between field and laboratory conditions will always occur, but the discrepancy is particularly large now. Revising tests to address these problems will be difficult for administrative, technical and practical reasons. According to Meier, the next generation of test procedures will probably need to combine hardware and software tests. In one approach, hardware tests could be conducted in a manner similar to current tests, except that measurements for more than one set of conditions would be taken to enable extrapolation of performance over a range of conditions. The software tests would involve presenting the microcontroller (via a direct connection to a computer in the testing facility) to thousands of different conditions and recording its responses. The results of the hardware and software tests would be combined to determine an overall energy efficiency score, upon which a new generation of labels and standards could be based. There are other possible approaches, and indeed several different approaches will probably be necessary for different appliances.

Revising the tests presents an excellent opportunity for countries to pursue coordination and harmonisation.

INTERNATIONAL CO-OPERATION

Chapter 1 described how labels and standards are being used by more and more governments to increase the efficiency of more and more products. As the programmes proliferate, the potential advantages of international co-operation become increasingly apparent. Several forms of co-operation are conceivable, including: *collaboration* in the design of tests, labels and standards; *co-ordination* of the programme implementation and monitoring efforts; *harmonisation* of test procedures; and *harmonisation* of the energy set points used in labels and standards.

Reasons for International Co-operation

The usefulness and feasibility of international co-operation varies from product to product, but there are five general benefits: greater market transparency, reduced costs for product testing and design, enhanced prospects for trade and technology transfer, reduced costs for developing government and utility efficiency programmes, and enhanced international procurement.

Greater Market Transparency

International co-operation would improve the comparability of information from market to market, or market transparency. This would enable consumers, producers, retailers, government and utilities to inform themselves better about more examples of products and component technologies. They could investigate how foreign models and technologies might function under local conditions, for example. With this information, governments and utilities could better design programmes that promote the most cost-effective available technologies for their markets.

Transparency would also give governments and utilities clearer, more independent information about technological capabilities and limits. This would improve their ability to work with manufacturers, both domestic and foreign, in developing more efficient products.

Reduced Costs for Product Testing and Design

If tests, labels and standards can be harmonised, the cost to the manufacturers of testing and design can be reduced. The current multiplicity of tests required by national programmes is very costly for manufacturers wishing to sell in more than one market. Moreover, the dissimilar national programmes increase design costs as well.

Enhanced Prospects for Trade and Technology Transfer

International co-operation would improve conditions for trade and technology transfer. Among other things, it would enlarge the energy-efficient segments of product markets. This applies not only to the products themselves, but to the component technologies as well. Larger markets would allow greater economies of scale and lower prices for more efficient products and component technologies and would increase the incentives for manufacturers to develop them. Harmonisation of tests and energy labels and standards would also discourage protectionist favouritism.

Reduced Costs for Developing Government and Utility Efficiency Programmes

International co-operation would assist governments and utilities to design, implement, and monitor efficiency programmes related to tests, labels and standards. By sharing data and analytical tasks, governments and utilities could reduce the cost of developing test protocols and analysing potential labelling and standards programmes. Moreover, reducing the number of demands made on manufacturers might make possible greater improvements in efficiency. In other words, fewer demands might allow stronger demands.

Also, internationally accepted analytical methods, test protocols, labels and standards, would be a model that other countries — be they developed, developing or transition economies — could use to develop efficiency programmes. The pace of market developments in some countries justify early actions to ensure a more sustainable pattern of development. The model not only would be a useful starting point for programme development and implementation, but also would increase the likelihood that such programmes are pursued in the first place. It is easier to implement these programmes if other countries are doing likewise. It is easier to follow suit than be first.

Enhanced International Procurement

International co-operation, if it leads to harmonised or compatible test protocols, could improve the energy efficiency of products developed and purchased through international procurement programmes. For example, common testing protocols would increase the number of potential suppliers that could compete for bulk purchase contracts issued by the World Bank and other development institutions. Likewise, common tests would raise the number of competitors for innovation procurement programmes, such as Golden Carrots contests. The greater level of competition in these cases would generate a wider variety of product and technology choices from which to choose the most cost-effective for the particular market being served.

Types of International Co-operation

As mentioned, several levels of co-operation are conceivable — collaboration in the design of tests, labels and standards; coordination of the programme implementation and monitoring efforts; harmonisation of test procedures; and harmonisation of the energy labelling and standards levels used in the various programmes.

Co-operation in the form of collaboration and coordination presents few, if any, disadvantages. Such efforts may slow programme development in some countries, but will no doubt speed development in others. Harmonisation of test protocols, labelling and standards, though, has a more fundamental potential weakness. Labels, targets, and regulatory standards might be set at sub-optimum levels if the regional and national differences are not properly assimilated. The issues associated with harmonisation are discussed in the next section.

Harmonisation of Test Protocols

Harmonisation of test protocols would bring four principal benefits. First, and foremost, it lays the ground work for reduced testing and compliance costs for manufacturers. If common test protocols are adopted, and trading partners grant mutual recognition of tests conducted in each others' jurisdictions, multiple testing of products could be eliminated or reduced. Second, common test protocols lay the ground for comparing the performance of products across national boundaries, so that consumers can be better informed of the range of product choices that could be available to them. Likewise, such comparisons could enable energy efficiency programme managers to choose from a wider range models when developing their promotion efforts. Third, common tests could encourage the transfer of more efficient components among manufacturers. Lastly, common test procedures would be a necessary first step if labels and standards were ever to be harmonised.

■ developing common definitions of energy use metrics, test methods and conditions, and product categories for energy test protocols,

- developing common definitions of performance metrics, adjustments for service features, and product categories for product characterisations,

If countries were to decide to harmonise their labelling and standards programmes, their differing, and sometimes firmly established, product test protocols would need to be reconciled. If parties cannot agree on common tests, they will find it nearly impossible to harmonise their systems of labels and standards. For international harmonisation of test protocols to work properly, they must take into account regional and national differences in: electricity, climate and local environments, product service features, and behavioural and product usage patterns.

Electricity — The supply current has different voltages and frequency around the world (e.g., 120V and 60 Hz in North America; 230V and 50 Hz in Europe), so testing is performed at these local electrical conditions. Appliances are manufactured to work at the local electrical conditions and must be tested according to the specified input requirements.

Climate and local environments — Local conditions affect the testing parameters of some products, in particular space heating and cooling products. For example, for room air conditioners, North America uses one set of conditions for temperature and humidity whereas most of the world uses the ISO protocol which allows for any of three possible sets of conditions. For central air conditioners and heat pumps, the difference in test protocols is greater — the United States uses a seasonal energy efficiency ration (or SEER) whereas the ISO protocol uses a single point rating. Local conditions regarding water hardness affects the testing of wet appliances.

Product service features — For example with refrigerators, there are multiple doors in Japan, multiple freezer compartment temperatures in Europe, and through-the-door features in the United States.

Behavioural and product usage patterns — For example, wash temperatures for dishwashers and clothes washers vary in different parts of the world — European temperatures tend to be higher than North American values.

The barriers to harmonisation can be overcome through definitions of product classes flexible enough to accommodate differences in product characteristics and usage. Take the example of room air conditioners. The ISO protocol allows for a rating under a choice of three operating conditions, one of which is identical to the US test protocol. Harmonisation could allow for the status quo, but also require all countries to provide a rating under a common operating condition, and others as they wish. Ideally, one condition would be sufficient, but the wide variation in climate across the countries utilizing air conditioners could make it difficult to agree on the one set of operating conditions.

Flexibility is also needed in international testing protocols to account for the energy use of special features, such as through the door ice makers on refrigerator/freezers and power drying cycles for dishwashers. Protocols should give credit to features that reduce energy use, for example, clothes washers that have higher spin speeds on the spin dry cycle take more moisture out of clothes, reducing the energy needed to dry them in a clothes dryer.

The timing of protocol harmonisation is hard to estimate because it depends very strongly upon the degree of agreement between the harmonising parties. In the current climate there is no necessity to harmonise protocols between the major markets; thus, it will only happen if all the parties agree. Assuming that agreement is possible protocol harmonisation could take as little as two years.

Harmonisation of Labels and Standards

Harmonisation of labels and standards would enhance the development energy efficiency programmes in the five ways mentioned earlier — greater market transparency, reduced costs for product testing and design, enhanced prospects for trade and technology transfer, reduced costs for developing government and utility efficiency programmes, and enhanced international procurement.

There are a number of factors that would complicate, and in some cases render infeasible, common labels and standards. First, differing socio-political attitudes toward voluntary vs. mandatory measures would need to be accommodated. Second, differing cost-effectiveness of labels and standards would need to be resolved. Regional and national differences in cost-effectiveness of labels and standards arise from the same factors that affect the appropriateness of tests described above: climate, product service characteristics, and behavioural and product usage patterns. But other factors are also involved: electricity and fuel prices, private and social discount rates and other economic factors, manufacturing costs, and the state of the art of the manufacturing industry. Also, in the case of labels, differences in consumers' perception and comprehension, which can vary from country to country, would need to be accommodated.

The perceived need for efficiency programmes such as regulatory standards varies to some degree with prevailing electricity and fuel prices. Regions with low energy prices and surplus capacity are generally less disposed toward efficiency measures. Additionally, the level of an efficiency code that is cost-effective is strongly dependent upon the price of energy (and also behavioural patterns and climate).

Policy preferences for mandatory and voluntary measures is another important factor in harmonising energy programmes. In some countries, such as Japan and Sweden, voluntary measures fit well with policy predilections. Achieving harmony among all stakeholders is a particularly important policy objective in this kind of environment. Therefore, it is undesirable to impose regulations on appliance and equipment manufacturers if effective voluntary measures can be agreed to. It should be possible for countries to co-operate on energy programmes regardless of whether they prefer mandatory or voluntary approaches to product labels, targets, and regulatory standards.

Product service characteristics and operating behaviour differences also affect the ability to harmonize performance specifications. For example, if clothes washers are used more often in some regions than others, more stringent efficiency standards would be economically justified in those regions of greater usage. There may be little to be gained by harmonising energy labels and standards across products that are very different, European models are generally smaller and offer fewer services than US models. Other parameters such as freezer temperature are also different in Europe and North America.

In short, harmonisation of labels and standards makes most sense for products in which product characteristics and usage patterns (behaviour) don't vary greatly from country to country, and where the level of efficiency that is economically justifiable is rather insensitive to energy prices.

Opportunities for International Harmonisation

Global harmonisation of test protocols and possibly regulatory standards for refrigerators and freezers would take a great amount of effort and a very long time. The net benefits of global regulatory standards is not clear. The potential gains by extending existing regulatory standards to new areas/regions may be offset by the regulatory standards being lower than they might otherwise be. Some experts feel harmonisation of testing procedures could be worthwhile. Others stress the opportunities for work without the need for fully harmonised test protocols, for example there are great opportunities for energy savings from refrigerators and freezers in China, India and the Central and Eastern European Economies. There is perhaps a greater need and net benefit with encouraging the development of "regional" regulatory standards, rather than global regulatory standards, given the different characteristics of products in each market.

Air-conditioners is a potential area for "regional" regulatory standards, in particular in South-East Asia. The attractiveness stems from the growing market, the similarity of testing protocols worldwide, and the product characteristics not varying greatly from country to country.

From the viewpoint of achieving early success in harmonisation of regulatory standards, efforts aimed at micro-wave ovens might be worthwhile. The test protocol is already the same throughout the world. There may be limited interest, though, because the magnitude of the energy saving potential in this area is considered small.

Wet appliances (clothes washing machines, clothes driers, and dishwashers) are a difficult area for harmonisation efforts, because, among other things, the energy use of these appliances is heavily influenced by behavioural characteristics. However, there might be opportunities for international co-operation of some other types, perhaps in sharing tasks in analytical efforts.

The U.S. EPA's Energy Star label is seen as a de facto "international" label for office equipment. One area of international co-operation might be IEA programme support for the Energy Star programme, in the form of administrative support, or perhaps in analytical support for updating the programme and expanding it into other areas. If a more activist role is envisioned, the IEA could organise government-industry roundtables on testing procedures and levels, and host negotiations on targets values.

CONCLUSIONS AND RECOMMENDATIONS

CONCLUSIONS

Energy efficiency labels and standards for appliances and equipment are playing key roles in governments' strategies to meet energy and environmental goals. They are already widely used to improve the efficiency of home appliances and office equipment, and are increasingly being implemented for electric motors, home electronics and lighting equipment. At present, labels are used in 37 countries; standards in 34 countries. The market influence of labels and standards is increasing as countries expand and strengthen their programmes, and as developing countries and as countries with economies in transition initiate new programmes.

Programmes around the world differ considerably because of market conditions, jurisdictional issues and policy preferences. In IEA countries, for example, various combinations of comparison labels, endorsement labels, minimum efficiency standards, moving average standards (such as Japan's Top-Runner scheme), target values (such as Switzerland's E-2000 programme) and negotiated agreements are used. This wide range of independent programmes opens up opportunities for improvement through international information exchange and collaboration.

Regrettably, there have been few studies of the *actual* results of the labels and standards programmes. Nonetheless, those studies that have been made show clearly that labels and standards, when well designed, can be effective in encouraging the development, marketing and sale of energy efficient products, without compromise to the products' services, performance and features. In addition, they enhance the effectiveness of other market transformation activities, such as targeted procurement, financial incentives, information, training and research and development.

Other studies, which focus on the *expected* results of the programmes, show opportunities for substantial energy savings and CO_2 emissions reductions at attractive costs. For example, a recent study of the U.S. appliance standards programme foresees total savings of 10.6 exajoules (EJ) of primary energy between 1990 and 2010. Annual energy savings, which vary as energy efficient appliances replace existing stock, peak in 2004 at 0.69 EJ, representing more than 3% of projected residential energy consumption in that year. Projected carbon reductions are approximately 9 Megatonnes (Mt) carbon per year from 2000 through 2010, an amount roughly equal to 4% of U.S. residential carbon emissions in 1990. The savings were found to be very cost effective. For consumers, the standards are expected to add $13 billion to the cost of appliances, but save $46 billion in energy consumption between 1990 and 2010. The Federal government's programme expenditures have been $200 million. Thus, $165 of consumer savings are expected for each dollar spent by the Federal government[24] (Koomey, 1998).

RECOMMENDATIONS

Given the potential for highly cost-effective energy savings and CO_2 reductions, labels and standards should be pursued. They are measures that should play a prominent role in any climate change package.

The complexities of the technologies, markets, legal systems and stakeholder interests related to appliances and equipment can make labels and standards programmes rather complicated to design. There are many tasks involved. There are, however, seven fundamental elements that should be addressed to some extent by every programme.

---

24 . *Monetary figures are in 1995 U.S. dollars, net present value calculated at 7% real discount rate.*

Table 6.1   Principle Programme Elements

	Elements (steps)	Goals
1	Preliminary assessment and priority setting	■ Strategic plan for market intervention, with well articulated goals ■ Recommendations for provisions of a framework law or decree ■ Recommendations for provisions of a framework law or decree. Heightened awareness among stakeholders of impending policy intervention
2	Political or legal authorisation and programme design procedures	■ Political legitimacy for energy-efficiency initiatives through demonstrated strength of political support and resolve ■ Clear programme objectives and boundaries, with clear lines of programme authority ■ An open and transparent process for programme design ■ Planning for coherent relationships with other relevant energy and non-energy policies
3	Priority refinement — selecting final products and instruments	■ A multi-year work plan, reflecting refined product priorities and a timetable for programme review and updates ■ Baseline forecasts of product purchases, product use rates, energy use, energy efficiency and CO_2 emissions for later evaluation efforts
4	Design — technical parameters and compliance deadlines	■ A set of technical parameters for each product chosen for intervention ■ A label design that it is clear, informative and attention-getting
5	Design — testing procedures	■ Test procedures that give accurate and reproducible data on energy use and performance for a wide range of product models and duty cycles. Procedures should be low-cost, easily adaptable to new product technologies or features and not act as barriers to trade
6	Design — administrative rules and conformity assessment	■ Solid programme credibility through the proof that rules are being followed ■ Data and procedures to provide assurance of programme conformance, and to allow credible, low-cost assessment of the programme's impact ■ Administration procedures that are simple, clear and transparent, with low costs to government and stakeholders ■ Laboratory accreditation procedures that have low costs and do not act as barriers to trade
7	Monitoring, evaluation and reporting	■ Solid credibility through public accountability for programmes' accomplishments ■ A programme that is cost-effective and relevant in the face of technological development and market trends ■ Low evaluation costs ■ Data on the impact of programmes for analytical forecasts

For successful labels and standards programmes, these elements should be addressed in a manner that results in:

■ coherent packages of multiple policy instruments,
■ open, transparent and systematic programme development procedures,
■ programme elements that reflect product and market realities,
■ solid programme credibility.

Coherent packages of multiple policy instruments

There are various ways to encourage the marketing and sales of more efficient appliances and equipment. No single policy instrument can realistically be expected to deliver all the potential cost-effective energy savings for a given product. It is thus necessary to implement packages of multiple policy instruments. But they must be coherent packages. The component instruments should complement and reinforce, not contradict, each other.

Open, transparent and systematic programme development procedures

There are two major problems in programme design — unclear priorities and discord among interested parties, known as "stakeholders". These issues can be detrimental to the design and operation of an effective labelling and standards programme. The best way to prevent them, or remedy them should they arise, is to establish open, transparent and systematic programme development procedures. Such procedures should incorporate *extensive stakeholder consultation* along with *thorough market and engineering analysis*. Carrying out these exercises in an open, transparent and predictable manner helps ensure that programmes embody consistent priorities and are developed in a manner consistent with technical, economic and commercial realities.

Stakeholder consultation also increases the chances that they will support the programme, and that programme requirements and targets are designed with cost-effective compliance in mind. Consultation among diverse stakeholders can also be a source of policy creativity, leading to new and better policy measures.

Thorough engineering and market analyses are vital to developing programmes with the right balance of impact and cost. But such analyses can be expensive and time-consuming. It is important therefore that they be conducted systematically, with transparent and robust methods. The goals should be timeliness and comprehensiveness to avoid overlooking opportunities, and realism with respect to different technical and market situations. To keep analytical costs low, the priority-setting phase should recognise and screen out less viable options from further consideration promptly.

Programme elements that reflect product and market realities

The principal programme elements — test protocols, labels, and standards — should be designed so that they fit the markets in which they will function. They should be as simple as possible, while taking due account of product and market complexities.

Test protocols — Energy-use test protocols are the cornerstone of all labelling and standards programmes. Test protocols encompass many features, including: an energy-use metric; depiction of the conditions under which energy use measurements are made; a performance metric and a rough-cut distinction between major product classes; allowable tolerances; and measuring-instrument specifications. An ideal test would:

- reflect actual usage conditions;
- yield repeatable, accurate results;
- accurately reflect the relative performance of different design options for a given appliance;

- cover a wide range of models within that category of appliance;
- be inexpensive;
- be easy to modify to accommodate new technologies or features;
- produce results that can be easily compared with results from other test procedures.

As these goals are in part contradictory, all energy test protocols are necessarily compromises. A test that aims to reproduce actual product usage conditions will probably be expensive and difficult to replicate. At a minimum, however, tests should rank different models' energy use in the same order as would be expected under field use conditions (Meier, 1997b).

Governments usually relinquish the responsibility for developing and maintaining test protocols to trade associations or national, regional or international standards organisations. But they are certainly free to advise the protocol-writing bodies of their preferences regarding the compromises to be made.

Labels — The chief purpose of information labels is to alert and inform consumers about the energy use and costs of their prospective product purchases. They can also protect consumers from inaccurate claims made by manufacturers and dealers and provide an information foundation for other energy efficiency measures. At a minimum, information labels should provide two services. They should make potential purchasers as aware of a product's energy performance as they are of its size, colour and purchase price. They should also convey accurate information that is easily compared among product models. To do this, labels must be visually striking, convey information in a quick and easily understandable way and be supported by promotion efforts and by trained salespersons.

Standards — There are various ways to structure the standards, but what is most important is to achieve the desired balance among the interests of consumers, manufacturers and society, at the lowest possible costs. Achieving this requires thorough engineering and market analyses, well informed by consultation of interested parties.

Solid programme credibility

Labels and standards must exhibit a high degree of credibility to be effective. Market actors and political interests must have confidence that the programmes are working well. It is *conformity assessment and enforcement systems* which can maintain credibility with programme participants; adequate *programme evaluation* can maintain credibility with the public, their government representatives and the programme personnel.

Conformity assessment and enforcement systems should entail testing, reporting and checking procedures, and penalties for non-compliance, that yield the right balance of credibility and cost. It is important that the systems are presented in a manner in which all programme participants understand their responsibilities.

Programme evaluation should provide coherent measurements and assessments of four major programme elements — programme inputs, programme outputs, programme outcomes and market outcomes (NRCan, 1996 and 1998). Each element, and the links between them, can give useful insights into how to improve programmes. The true market outcome (the actual changes in energy use or CO_2 emissions compared to what would have occurred in the absence of the particular programme) is certainly the most important element. But direct measurement of the actual energy savings or CO_2 emissions resulting from labels and standards (with large scale in-field monitoring) is difficult and expensive. In fact, given the nature of measuring energy savings (or absence of energy use) from a hypothetical business-as-usual baseline, it is probably impossible to know the true market outcomes of labels and standards. For that matter, it may be impossible to gauge the true market outcome of *any* energy efficiency policy. It is therefore necessary to find a combination of measurements and supportable assumptions from which a low-cost, sufficiently-certain picture of market effects can be drawn.

Programme evaluation is made somewhat easier if the programmes are designed from their inception to be evaluated. In this regard, there should be: clear programme goals, co-ordinated data collection, a business-as-usual baseline, integrated planning and evaluation, and correlation with end-use indicators.

Clear programme goals	Programmes should have explicit, and to the extent possible, measurable, goals against which performance can be measured.
Co-ordinated data collection	The data needed for programme evaluation is often similar to those required for programme implementation. From the outset of the programme, the data activities for both the implementation and evaluation phases should be co-ordinated in order to reduce the overall data collection and analysis effort.
A business-as-usual baseline	Programmes should be established against the background of a credible business-as-usual baseline of energy use and greenhouse gas emissions with relevant corrections for business cycles, economic trends and technological change.
Integrated planning and evaluation	Planning and evaluation are closely related activities, which must inform each other. Planning involves setting targets that are realistic for a given policy goal. Evaluation involves judging actual programme performance against those targets. The evaluation results should be fed back into the planning system in the form of improved bases for planning future programmes and, perhaps, revising targets for the current programme.

(continued)

Correlation with end-use indicators	In-depth evaluations, though expensive, can ultimately save governments money by increasing programme performance and efficiency. Techniques for correlating evaluation results with less costly energy-use indicators should be developed in order to achieve the same programme performance, efficiency and credibility benefits with fewer in-depth evaluations.

Future energy test protocols

Microcontrollers in combination with sensors are becoming commonplace in appliances and equipment of all sorts. These new control technologies present two major challenges to energy test protocols. First, they can be used to circumvent labels and standards, by being programmed to operate with uncharacteristically low energy use while undergoing standard tests. Second, existing test procedures can discourage the introduction of legitimate, energy-saving technologies relying on microcontroller technology (Meier, 1998). Increasingly, energy test protocols will need to be revised to take account of the capabilities of these technologies. The required revisions present an excellent opportunity to pursue coordination and harmonisation of energy test procedures on an international scale.

International co-operation

As labelling and standards programmes proliferate, the potential advantages of international co-operation become increasingly apparent. Increased international co-operation on ratings, labels, targets and regulatory standards could increase effectiveness and reduce costs. Several forms of co-operation are conceivable, including: *collaboration* in the analytical methods for designing tests, labels and standards; *co-ordination* of the programme implementation and monitoring efforts; *harmonisation* of test procedures; and *harmonisation* of the energy set points used in labels and standards.

The usefulness and feasibility of international co-operation varies from product to product, but there are five general benefits: 1) greater market transparency, 2) reduced costs for product testing and design, 3) enhanced prospects for trade and technology transfer, 4) reduced costs for developing government and utility efficiency programmes, and 5) enhanced international procurement.

The benefits of the *reduced costs for developing government and utility efficiency programmes* will become increasingly important as more and more developing countries and countries with economies in transition seek to combat climate change and alleviate energy shortages. International collaboration on labels and standards would encourage these countries to taken action and would help them reduce programme costs. One approach might be to develop models of internationally-accepted analytical methods, test protocols, labels and standards for these countries to use and adapt to their situation. The model elements would not only be a useful starting point for programme development and implementation, but would also increase the likelihood that such programmes are pursued in the first place. It is easier to implement these programmes if other countries are doing likewise.

APPENDIX A
OVERVIEW OF CURRENT LABELS AND STANDARDS PROGRAMMES IN IEA COUNTRIES

AUSTRALIA

As of June 2000, Australia uses labels and standards on the following products:

Labels and Standards	refrigerators and freezers
Labels only	clothes dryers; clothes washers; dishwashers; gas central heaters; gas space heaters; gas water heaters; and room air conditioners
Standards only	electric storage water heaters
Endorsement Labels	office equipment

Information Labels

Appliance labelling in Australia has its roots at the state level. It was first proposed in New South Wales (NSW) and Victoria, the country's two most populous states, in the late 1970s. Initial proposals met with considerable resistance from the appliance industry, on the grounds that labelling programmes should be uniform nationally rather than State-specific and voluntary rather than mandatory. To ensure national uniformity, the NSW government referred the matter to the joint Commonwealth States council of energy ministers. Despite three years of negotiations, the government and industry could not agree on a mutually satisfactory voluntary labelling programme (Harrington, 1997). In 1985, the governments of NSW and Victoria instituted a mandatory energy labelling scheme on their own. As NSW and Victoria accounted for 60% of total appliance sales, the bilateral scheme became a de-facto national programme. Labels for refrigerators and freezers become effective in 1986, and labels for air conditioners and dishwashers were introduced in 1987 and 1988. After a change of government in NSW in 1989, Victoria pressed on alone, and implemented labelling for clothes dryers in 1989 and clothes washers in 1990. In the following year, South Australia introduced labelling for the same five classes of home appliances. By 1994, almost all Australian states had in place energy efficiency labelling for refrigerators, dishwashers, clothes washers, clothes dryers and room air conditioners making it a truly national programme. Today, appliance labelling is co-ordinated at the national level. Nationally-consistent laws on appliance efficiency labelling came in to effect in 1999 (NAEEEC, 1999).

Currently, the design and star rating algorithms of the labels are currently being reviewed to ensure their currency, usefulness to consumers and technical rigour. The proposed launch date of the new labels is in 2000. Australia has also adopted an endorsement labelling (Energy Star) programme for office equipment.

Gas water heaters, space heaters and central heaters are also labelled, under a separate programme administered by the Australian Gas Association. An extension of this programme to include gas and electric cooking and electric storage, solar, and heat pump water heating systems is being examined.

Labelling data are subject to check-testing as a means of quality assurance for the program. The labels are supported by guidebooks listing all the labelled appliances and other promotional material produced by the government and by the electric utilities (Harrington, 1994 & 1997).

Standards

The Commonwealth, State and Territory governments of Australia committed themselves in the 1992 *National Greenhouse Response Strategy* to the development, in consultation with the manufacturing industry, of minimum energy performance standards (MEPS) for domestic electrical appliances, beginning with refrigerators, freezers and electric storage water heaters. In 1995, Australian energy ministers agreed to implement MEPS for refrigerators and electric storage water heaters effective in October 1999. Based on a statistical analysis of the Australian market, the standards are intended to reduce the average sales-weighted energy consumption of new models by between 11 per cent and 18 per cent compared to the Australian new-model stock in 1992 (GWA 1993). MEPS levels will be reviewed after 5 years. MEPS for packaged air conditioners, lighting ballasts and motors have been proposed, but not yet authorised (NAEEEC, 1999).

National Co-ordination

Australia's energy efficiency labelling and standards programmes are co-ordinated at the national level — through the National Appliance and Equipment Energy Efficiency Committee (NAEEEC), comprised of officials from the Commonwealth, State and Territory government agencies plus a representative from New Zealand, responsible for product energy efficiency.[25] Political support at this level was shown in the 1998 National Greenhouse Strategy, which states that "improvements in the energy efficiency of domestic appliances and commercial and industrial equipment will be promoted by extending and enhancing the effectiveness of existing energy labelling and minimum energy performance standards programs." This will be pursued by:

---

25. Established under the auspices of the 1992 National Greenhouse Response Strategy, NAEEEC reports to the Australian and New Zealand Minerals and Energy Council (ANZMEC), which is made up of the Ministers with portfolio responsibility in this field.

- developing MEPS for a broader range of new appliances and equipment;

- regulating or developing codes of practice to ensure the adoption of energy performance standards;

- revising the technical framework of the labelling programme to keep pace with improvements in product efficiencies including "super efficient" appliances;

- working with industry to improve gas appliance MEPS and labelling programs; and

- ensuring consistency of approach between Australia and New Zealand wherever possible.

The National Appliance and Equipment Energy Efficiency Program, issued in 1999, sets out the policy framework for Australia's labelling and standards programme in the next several years. One of its aims is that Australia match the world's "best practice" standards. The standards of the country's major trading partners will be reviewed, and the most stringent will become the basis for new Australian standards (NAEEEC, 1999). The review of refrigerator and freezer standards has already begun. Preliminary indications are the that the U.S. 2001 refrigerator and freezer standards are the toughest. If this is borne out, the next round of Australian standards will be based on the U.S. standards after suitable adjustments for climate, test procedures and performance prerequisites (Appliance Efficiency, 2000).

The new national approach to appliance efficiency relies heavily on Standards Australia. The organisation issues a two part "standard" (called a protocol here to avoid confusion with minimum energy performance standards) to define each energy labelling and standards rule. Part 1 of each protocol defines the test procedures for measuring energy consumption and sets minimum performance criteria which appliances must meet. The minimum performance requirements include temperature operation specifications for refrigerators and minimum wash performance for dishwashers and clothes washers. They are important consumer protection features of the Australian programme, preventing appliances from claiming low energy consumption because of poor overall performance. A programme of check tests against these requirements are conducted on a regular basis by state and territory governments, who contract accredited laboratories to undertake the tests (Harrington, 1997). Part 2 of the protocol contains the detailed technical requirements for the energy labels and standards. While Part 2 is drafted by the relevant Standards Australia committee (to ensure a seamless interface with Part 1), it is under the joint control of the State energy regulators who have to approve the standard prior to its publication. Part 2 includes data on how to calculate star ratings and the comparative energy consumption (the energy number that appears on the label), details on the number of units to be tested, minimum performance requirements, application forms, check testing procedures, the design and shape of the energy label and how the label is to be affixed to the appliance. Part 2 also describes the applicable minimum energy performance standards.

The new programme structure provides a "one-stop energy efficiency shop" for industry and regulators, addressing not only testing and performance requirements, but also energy labelling and minimum energy performance requirements. As of mid-1998, protocols for all five of the labelled appliance types have been published in the new two part format. All Australian energy labelling protocols are now jointly published with Standards New Zealand.

Though efforts are now being led at the national level, individual States and Territories are still responsible for legislation, regulation and associated administration. State-based legislation is necessary because the Australian constitution gives Australian States clear responsibility for resource management issues, including energy. The regulations specify the general requirements for the energy labelling of appliances, including offences and penalties if a party does not comply with the requirements. They have, however, little technical content regarding requirements for energy labelling — they will merely refer to the relevant Australian Standard (Part 2) for the technical requirements for each appliance type. The States are currently in the process of harmonising their programmes, by repealing their existing regulations and replacing these with model regulations. The prospect for state variations with the laws are thereby minimised.

CANADA

Canada has one of the most extensive appliance and equipment energy labelling and standards programme in the world. As of June 2000, eight appliances are required to carry energy information labels, and twenty-eight products are required to meet minimum energy efficiency standards.

Labels and Standards	clothes dryers (electric, standard and compact); clothes washers; dishwashers; freezers; integrated stacking washer-dryers; ranges (electric); refrigerators; and room air conditioners
Standards only	boilers (gas and oil); dehumidifiers; fluorescent lamp ballasts; furnaces (gas and oil); general service fluorescent lamps; general service incandescent reflector lamps; ground- or water-source heat pumps; ice-makers; internal water-loop heat pumps; large air conditioners, heat pumps and condensing units; motors (electric); packaged terminal air conditioners and heat pumps; ranges (gas); single-phase and three-phase single-package central air conditioners and heat pumps; single-phase and three-phase split-system central air conditioners and heat pumps; and water heaters (electric, gas and oil)

Information Labels

Canada introduced the world's first energy information label, the EnerGuide label, for household appliances and other energy-using equipment in May 1978. EnerGuide is a federal regulatory programme that requires dealers (manufacturers, importers, sellers and lessors) to affix labels on their products showing each model's annual energy consumption and how it compares to similar models on the Canadian market. Since federal jurisdiction in energy is limited to international and inter-provincial commerce, EnerGuide applies only to products imported into Canada and/or shipped between provinces, and not to products manufactured and sold within a single province. Nonetheless, given the scope of the markets, the transborder shipment requirement affects virtually all prescribed products.

EnerGuide was initiated under the authority of the Consumer Packaging and Labelling Act, with the objective of encouraging consumers to purchase the most energy-efficient household appliances, and protecting consumers against exaggerated claims made by manufacturers and other dealers (CADDET, 1997). Consumer and Corporate Affairs Canada, with the help of Natural Resources Canada (NRCan), administered the programme from its inception until the end of 1992. Since 1993, EnerGuide has had its statutory authority in the 1992 Energy Efficiency Act and the subsequent Energy Efficiency Regulations, and has been administered in full by NRCan.

In the programme's initial years, the schedule for labelling products was determined by the development of testing standards by the Canadian Standards Association (CSA). Labelling began for refrigerators in 1978, freezers in 1979, clothes washers in 1980, dishwashers in 1980, electric ranges (ovens and cooktops) in 1981 and clothes dryers in 1982. During this period, independent product testing was not required. Conformance monitoring was left to market competitors, who were expected to call attention to non-compliant products in the market.

Under the Energy Efficiency Act and Regulations, the EnerGuide programme was enhanced in several important ways. First, room air conditioners and integrated over/under clothes washer-dryers were added to the list of products requiring labels. Second, following consumer focus group studies, the labels were changed to improve the clarity of the information presented. The labels now indicate the product's ranking on an energy efficiency scale among similar models available in Canada. Third, products are now required to be tested by independent accredited laboratories, with the test results sent to NRCan. Fourth, NRCan is authorised to conduct spot tests in order to ensure truthfulness of the information on the labels. And finally, it is the product dealers that have been made responsible for ensuring that an EnerGuide label is affixed to each piece of regulated equipment in Canada.

Products required bear the EnerGuide label, are selected in consultation with stakeholders. The criteria for deciding if the EnerGuide label should be mandatory on a product is that it should be seen by potential buyers at the point of sale.[26] Marketplace monitoring and enforcement systems are implemented through audits on the frequency of labelling. NRCan supports the EnerGuide programme through directories for consumers, information and education campaigns, and training for retail sales staff. The campaigns, involving publications, media releases and exhibits, seek to foster consumer understanding of the EnerGuide label and the benefits of energy efficiency. The training programmes, developed by NRCan in collaboration with its strategic allies (provincial governments, utilities, and industry, consumer and standards

---

26. The voluntary use of the label has been extended to furnaces and being used in company documentation, the mostly likely place that consumers would see it.

organisations), endeavour to teach retail salespeople how to use the EnerGuide label. Major electric utilities and manufacturers are now considering implementing training programmes themselves (NRCan, 1998). In 1999, mandatory labels were developed for automobiles and buildings.

Standards

Provincial governments in Canada have used minimum energy efficiency standards to improve the average efficiency of equipment and appliances sold and leased in their jurisdictions since the late 1980s. Such standards were implemented in Ontario (1988), British Columbia (1990), Quebec (1992), Nova Scotia (1991) and New Brunswick (1995). At the federal level, the 1992 Energy Efficiency Act authorised the Governor in Council to "make regulations ... prescribing energy efficiency standards for energy-using products or prescribed classes of energy-using products," which were defined as "any manufactured product designed to operate using electricity, oil, natural gas or any other form or source of energy or to be used as a door system or window system." NRCan developed the regulations, and the first federal energy efficiency standards took effect in February 1995.

As with the EnerGuide programme, the federal appliance standards apply only to products imported into Canada and/or shipped between provinces. However, Ontario, British Columbia, Quebec, Nova Scotia and New Brunswick have continued to regulate most of the same products. Unlike the federal regulations, the provincial standards apply to products manufactured and sold within a single province, in addition to products coming from elsewhere. In essence, the federal standards apply at the borders, and the provincial standards apply at the point of sale. The provincial regulations sometimes differ from the federal ones or apply to other products, but in most cases, they are "mirrors" of the federal standards, resulting nearly uniform standards throughout the country.

NRCan takes provincial regulations into account when drafting national requirements. Its efforts to serve as a harmonising force for energy efficiency regulations within Canada have generally been well-received, since the provinces recognise that the interests of all parties are better served by working toward regulatory consistency from coast to coast (Des Rosiers, 1997).

Canada relies on the National Standards System to support the development and implementation of energy efficiency regulations. The custodian of this system is the Standards Council of Canada, a federal Crown corporation that has the authority to accredit standards writing, testing and certification organisations. Accredited organisations (such as the Canadian Standards Association International) develop national consensus on energy-consumption test methods and may, but usually do not, recommend minimum performance standards for a range of products. The test methods and performance standards may be formally adopted by governments through citation in a regulation. The consensus-building approach of the National Standards System provides NRCan with an important communication and consultation vehicle for discussing proposed standards (Des Rosiers, 1997).

Influence of U.S. Programmes

Most of Canada's energy efficiency standards are set at levels consistent with those in the United States, though the approaches of the two countries to setting the stringency levels are somewhat different. Canada bases its minimum energy performance requirements on actual products available in the market. The range of product efficiencies in the market establishes the boundaries within which efficiency options are analysed and decided upon. This contrasts with the more stringent U.S. approach, where regulations are based on what is technologically possible and economically justifiable.

Theoretically, this would imply that Canadian standards would tend to be less stringent than those in the United States. However, the Canadian regulatory process and markets are greatly influenced by the American situation. The more stringent American regulations are felt in the Canadian market because of cross-border trade and the multinational appliance and equipment manufacturers operating on both sides of the border (Des Rosiers, 1997).

CZECH REPUBLIC AND HUNGARY

The Czech Republic and Hungary are among the ten Central and Eastern European (CEE) states that have announced their desire to join the European Union, and which have begun developing labelling and standards in line with the EU regulations as part of the accession process. The Czech Republic is currently preparing legislation that would adopt all of the EU labels and standards. In Hungary, energy labelling and standards of household electric refrigerators took effect in 1998, and labelling of clothes washers and dryers were implemented by December 1999. So far, three countries (Bulgaria, Hungary and Poland) have enacted legislation concerning both labelling and refrigerator standards; two other countries (Lithuania and Romania) have enacted just labelling legislation (Appliance Efficiency, 1999) (Dašek, 1999) (IEA, 1999).

EUROPEAN UNION

As of June 2000, the EU requires labels on seven products and has standards on two products and negotiated agreements on three products.

Labels and Standards	refrigerators; freezers
Labels only	clothes (tumble) dryers; clothes washers; clothes washer-dryers, dishwashers; and lamps
Standards only	hot-water boilers
Negotiated Agreements	clothes washers; televisions; videocassette recorders and audio equipment

Information Labels

Though appliance labels were used in several European countries as early as the mid-1970s, widespread use began only in the 1990s with the implementation of the European Union programme.

France enacted a law allowing the government to develop mandatory labelling of energy consumption information on every "energy consuming apparatus" in 1974, and introduced compulsory labelling of energy consumption for all heating units, boilers, refrigerators, washing machines, televisions, ranges and ventilation equipment in 1976. The legislation obliged the manufacturers to provide the label but did not require retailers to display it, so the label was generally only seen when the consumer opened the appliance packaging after the purchase. (Waide, 1995) Moreover, there were no rigorous efforts to enforce the regulations. (Wilson, 1989)

West Germany held discussions on a system of product information to promote energy efficiency and assist consumer purchasing decisions in the 1970s, and formed the German Society of Product Improvement (DGPI) to design and implement a suitable system of energy efficiency labelling in 1978. (Waide, 1995) In 1980, manufacturers agreed to an informal voluntary agreement to label refrigerators, dishwashers, and electric and gas ovens (Wilson, 1989). The labelling scheme, which applied only to products manufactured domestically, not to imports, was supplemented by the testing and reporting of appliance efficiency data by an independent foundation, Stiftung Warentest (IEA, 1989).

Denmark passed the "Indication by Labelling of Energy Conservation Act" in 1982, but by 1989 had only adopted labels for ovens

Interest in appliance labels at the European Union (EU)[27] level began in May 1976, when the Council of Ministers issued a recommendation to Member States to introduce energy efficiency labelling schemes, following a single EU-wide approach, for certain electrical household appliances[28] (GWA, 1991). Soon afterwards, the EU's Rational Use of Energy Programme initiated studies on appliance energy labelling, and CENELEC[29] was charged with the development of testing methods. These efforts led to the 1979 Directive 79/530/EEC on the "indication by labelling of the energy consumption of household appliances," a framework directive setting out the general requirements for appliance energy labelling within Member States. The specific labelling requirements for each type of appliance were to be laid out in separate, forthcoming, implementing directives. However, only one such implementing directive — 79/531/EEC, for electric ovens — was ever issued. That more implementation directives were never forthcoming appears to

---

27. At the time, the European Union was called the European Economic Community (EEC).

28. 76/496/EEC: Council recommendation of 4 May 1976 on the rational use of energy for electrical household appliances.

29. The EU's test protocols are the responsibility of the European Committee for Standardisation (CEN) and European Electrotechnical Committee for Standardisation (CENELEC), which are federations of national standards institutes from the nations of the European Economic Area (the European Union and the European Free Trade Area, except Switzerland). The establishment of these standards agencies was an important component of the European market harmonisation process. The Treaty of Rome, the founding agreement of the European Union, established that any good which is lawfully produced and sold in one Member State should be eligible to be freely transported and sold in all other Member States without being further modified, tested, certified, renamed or otherwise changed (Article 30). By law, CEN and CENELEC's technical standards must be based on the international standards of the International Organisation for Standardisation (ISO) and the International Electrotechnical Commission (IEC).

have been caused by a mixture of apathy, technical disagreements, and opposition from individual countries (Waide, 1995).

The 1979 framework directive gave Member States the option of issuing their own compulsory labelling schemes, but required national schemes to follow the format prescribed in any of the associated implementing directives. It rendered existing national schemes, such as the French one, potentially illegal because they did not conform to the specifications of the framework directive. It also discouraged the drafting of new national schemes because they might contravene future implementation directives.

Denmark's decision to implement a mandatory energy labelling scheme for household appliances in 1990 broke the deadlock of inaction between the European Commission and the Member States. When, as required by law,[30] Denmark notified the Commission of its intention to implement its scheme, the Commission was obligated to decide whether the scheme was consistent with EU rules. Such a decision involves investigating whether the proposed scheme presents an obstacle to free trade between Member States and also whether implementation on a EU-wide scale make sense. Accordingly, the Commission requested that Denmark defer its legislation for a year during which time the Commission proposed to issue a draft Directive for a harmonised Community-wide mandatory labelling scheme. The revised framework directive (92/75/EEC) for mandatory energy labelling of household appliances was agreed in 1992.[31] The new directive cancelled the 1979 framework directive (79/530/EEC), and took into its own purview the existing implementing directive (79/531/EEC) on electric ovens. To date, six implementing directives have been

---

30. The 1986 Single European Act and the resulting legislation for the Single European Market, Directive 83/189/EEC, stipulate that any country wishing to implement new rules which may affect trade between Member States must notify the European Commission, and authorise the Commission to either block the proposed rules for a six-month period or for one year, provided it releases its own proposal for harmonised legislation.

31. Council Directive 92/75/EEC of 22 September 1992 on the indication by labelling and standard product information of the consumption of energy and other resources by household appliances.

issued under the 1992 framework (Table A1.1). The labelling requirements only become mandatory in Member States when the governments have transposed the directives into national law.

Table A1.1 EC Implementing Directives Issued Under the 1992 Framework Directive

Appliance	Directive	Issue date	Effective date
Refrigerators	94/2/EC	21 January 1994	1 January 1995
Washing machines	95/12/EC	23 May 1995	1 April 1996
Tumble dryers	95/13/EC	23 May 1995	1 April 1996
Combined washer-dryers	96/60/EC	19 September 1996	1 August 1997
Dishwashers	97/17/EC, amended by 1999/9/EC	16 April 1997	1 July 1998
Lamps	98/11/EC	27 January 1998	1 July 1999

It is the responsibility of each individual Member State to translate directives into law, take all necessary measures to ensure that all suppliers and dealers in their territory fulfil their obligations and ensure that the labelling scheme is accompanied by educational and promotional information campaigns aimed at encouraging more responsible use of energy by private customers. Initial indications are that there are great differences in the degree to which Member States enforce and support the labelling programme.

Standards

Appliance efficiency standards have been discussed in several individual Member States, but never actually implemented. EU standards for domestic gas- or oil-fired hot-water boilers were adopted in 1992 and become effective 1 January 1998. Consideration of additional standards was prompted, as in the case of labels, by a proposed unilateral action by a Member State. In January 1992, the Netherlands notified the Commission of its intention to introduce domestic minimum efficiency standards for refrigerators. The Commission reviewed the Dutch proposal and blocked it on the grounds that unilateral standards would contravene the free-trade terms of the single European market (Waide, 1997). To help develop its required counter proposal, the Commission hired a consortium of national energy and environmental agencies, later known as the Group for Efficient Appliances (GEA), to conduct an analysis and make recommendations on appropriate standards levels. Based on this analysis, the Commission issued a proposed directive on refrigerator efficiency standards in November 1994. The proposed directive was debated and revised by the European Parliament and the Council of Ministers, and Directive 96/57/EC on regulatory standards for refrigerators was approved on 3 September 1996, and took effect 3 September 1999. The standards exclude the majority of D, E, F and G class refrigerators from sale.

In June 1999, the Commission sent to the Parliament and Council a proposal for mandatory energy efficiency standards for fluorescent lighting ballasts. There have been studies and technical proposals for EU standards on other products, namely clothes washers and dryers, but none have been enacted.

Unlike the labelling situation, there is no framework legislation giving the Commission or other competent body the authority to introduce or revise efficiency standards on an on-going basis. Instead, for mandatory minimum energy efficiency standards to be passed it is necessary to seek separate approval on an appliance-by-appliance basis from the Council and the Parliament. In the future, the Commission intends to focus on negotiating voluntary agreements before developing additional regulatory standards (IEA 1994) (Waide, 1997).

Negotiated Agreements

There have also been attempts to improve appliance efficiencies in a non-regulatory manner. In January 1980, the German Federal Ministry of Economic Affairs reached an agreement with appliance manufacturers to improve the efficiency of specific energy-intensive products by up to 20 per cent by 1985 (IEA, 1989). The appliance efficiency goals were twice increased voluntarily by the appliance industry, in order to pre-empt government regulation.

In August 1994, Denmark notified the European Commission that it intended to establish domestic standards for energy efficiency standards of clothes washers and dishwashers (Turiel, 1995). The Commission rejected the proposal on some technical points, the principal one being that the standards were defined in terms of an outdated energy test protocol (Waide, 1997). The Commission had already contracted members of the GEA to conduct analysis of wet appliances (Waide, 1997). The GEA study was completed in June 1995, and the Commission used the results to pursue voluntary agreements with the European Federation of Domestic Appliance Manufacturers (CECED) to improve the energy efficiency of washing machines and dishwashers.

The CECED voluntary agreement on clothes washers, announced in October 1997, seeks to improve the European average consumption of new models by 20 per cent (in relation to the new models of 1994) by the end of 2000. It allows for sales of higher consumption machines in Southern countries to be offset by the marketing of more efficient appliances in the Northern countries. The first stage phased out clothes washers in the label classes G, F, and E by the end of 1997; the second stage seeks to phase out machines in class D having spin speeds greater than 600 rpm or capacities greater than 3 Kg by the end of 2000. In addition, the agreement contains some "soft targets" relating to certain features that may only be appropriate for certain groups of customers or regions, or which present particular marketing problems (Bertoldi, 1997) (Meli, 1997).

The European Commission is pursuing energy efficiency improvements on other appliances as well. Agreements have also been negotiated with European Association of Consumer Electronics Manufacturers (EACEM) to cut the power consumption of televisions, videocassette recorders and audio equipment when they are in standby mode (EWWE, 17 Oct 97). The Commission is continuing to pursue negotiated agreements on dishwashers, domestic electric storage water heaters, electric motors, external power supplies and set top boxes (Bertoldi, 1999) (Meli, 1999).

JAPAN

The centrepiece of Japan's appliance and equipment efficiency programme is the Top-Runner standards scheme.

Top Runner — Standards and Endorsement Labels	passenger cars and trucks, air conditioners, refrigerators, fluorescent lights, televisions, videocassette recorders, photocopiers, computers and magnetic hard-disk drives

Information Labels

Japan has an energy efficiency labelling scheme under the Law Concerning Rational Use of Energy (known as the Energy Conservation Law) passed in 1979. The law obliges manufacturers and importers of energy-consuming equipment to indicate the energy efficiency of their products. Cases of non-compliance are addressed through recommendations, orders and public announcements issued by the Minister of International Trade and

Industry. Manufacturer and/or importers who fail to obey the orders are subject to penalties.

In addition, a voluntary labelling scheme will be introduced in the summer of 2000. These new labels indicate, with a symbolic mark, the ratio of the product model's energy efficiency and the Top-Runner efficiency standard. If an appliance meets the standard, the manufacturer and/or importer is free to choose the appropriate colour of the label. By using this method, consumers can compare the efficiency of appliances, in a relative and quantitative way, at a glance.

Standards (Top-Runner)

The Energy Conservation Law requires manufacturers and importers of "designated machines" to make efforts to improve the energy efficiency of their machines (APEC, 1994). Under the Law, equipment is "designated" if it meets three requirements: high saturation, large energy consumption, and in particular need of performance improvement (Nakagami, 1997). For such equipment, the Minister establishes and publishes judgement standards used to set weighted-average energy-efficiency targets to be met in future years. Japan's standards specify lower limits for the average energy efficiency of each manufacturer's and importer's shipments in each product category. In this respect, they differ from the appliance standards in most other countries, which set minimum efficiency levels for individual appliances. If the actual energy efficiency of a manufacturer's or importer's products is lower than the target value, the Minister may make recommendations for enhancing the efficiency of subsequent production. If the manufacturer or importer does not comply with the recommendation, further action such as public notification or, under certain circumstances, issuing an order to implement the measures may be taken (APEC, 1994).

In 1979, Japan listed two household appliances — refrigerators and air conditioners (non-heat pump, cooling only types) — as designated equipment, and issued judgement standards for their improvement.[32] For refrigerators, manufacturers and importers were required to achieve an average 20 per cent efficiency improvement (based on a weighted average of energy consumption) over the consumption rate for the 1978 "cooling year" (October 1977 through September 1978). This improvement was to be made by no later than the end of the 1983 cooling year (i.e., by 30 September 1983). All domestic manufacturers met the efficiency improvement target. In December 1983, the "designated" status was removed from refrigerators, because the desired efficiency had been surpassed, and further technological improvements were thought unrealistic (Iwamoto, 1992). There was also concern that manufacturers could not eliminate chlorofluorocarbons (CFCs) from refrigerators and improve energy efficiency at the same time (Nakagami, 1997). For air conditioners, manufacturers and importers were required to achieve an average 17 per cent efficiency improvement over the consumption rate for the 1978 cooling year. This improvement was to be made by no later than the end of the 1983 cooling year. The original goal of 17 per cent was surpassed in 1984, but additional improvements were perceived as attainable, so the designated status was kept in place (Wilson, 1989).

The 1993 revisions to the Energy Conservation Law granted the Minister new enforcement authority regarding security measures on labelling of energy efficiency and other information, strengthened the standards for cooling-only air conditioners and passenger cars, and issued new standards for:

- Heat pump air conditioners (dual use, heating and cooling)
- Fluorescent lamps
- Televisions

---

32. Gasoline engine cars for ten or fewer passengers were also designated.

- Photocopiers
- Computers
- Magnetic hard-disk drives.

The 1998 revisions to the Energy Conservation Law strengthened the penalties for not meeting the standards by setting new fines for manufacturers and importers of appliances in non-compliance with the Government instructions. The revisions also established the Top-Runner standards programme, which sets the targets for the weighted-average energy efficiency of each manufacturer's and importer's shipments in predefined product categories to the level of the most energy-efficient model in each category on the current market. That is today's best model sets tomorrow's standards. The products included in the Top-Runner programme are: passenger cars and trucks, air conditioners, refrigerators, fluorescent lights, televisions, video cassette recorders (VCRs), photocopiers, computers and magnetic hard-disk drives. The targets are set according to categories of types, configurations and capacities of the products. For example, there are thirty-two different target levels pertaining air conditioners, differentiated by two principal types (heat pump, cooling-only), five configurations (e.g. direct blow/window, direct blow/wall mounted, and duct type) and five cooling capacities (ranging from 2.5 to 28.0 kW).[33] Equipment with highly specialised uses, unconfirmed measurement and efficiency evaluation methods or low market penetration rates are not subject to the standards. The improvement rates of energy efficiency (weighted according to 1997 product category shares) and the years they are to be met are shown in Table A1.2.

---

33. *Some air conditioner categories encompass more than one capacity level, so there are fewer targets than the combination of types, configurations and capacities would suggest.*

Table A1.2 Energy Efficiency Target Levels of the Top-Runner
Programme.

Product	Standards Levels	Units	Improvement rate of energy efficiency (%)	Target deadline (fiscal year)
Automobiles				
Gasoline, passenger cars	6.4 – 21.2	km/l	22.8 (vs. FY1995)	2010
Gasoline, trucks (<2.5 t)	9.3 – 20.2	km/l	13.2 (vs. FY1995)	2010
Diesel, passenger cars	8.7 – 18.9	km/l	14.9 (vs. FY1995)	2005
Diesel, trucks (<2.5 t)	9.9 – 17.7	km/l	6.5 (vs. FY1995)	2005
Refrigerators	varies by volume	kWh/year	30.4	2004
Air conditioners				
Heat pump	2.85 – 5.27	COP*	62.8	2004 (cooling year)**
Cooling-only	2.47 – 3.64	COP*	14.6	2007 (cooling year)
Fluorescent lights	49.0 – 86.5	lm/W	16.6	2005
Televisions	varies by screen size	kWh/year	16.4	2003
VCRs (stand-by power use)	1.7 – 4.0	W	58.7	2003
Photocopiers	varies by copy rate	Wh/h	30.1	2006
Computers	00065 – 21	W/MTOPS***	82.6	2005
Magnetic hard-disk drives	varies by rpm	W/GB	78.0	2005

Source: MITI, 1999.

* Coefficient of Performance (COP) = cooling or heating capacity divided by input power.

** The target year of heat pumps except direct blow/wall mounted type (<4kW) is 2007 cooling year.

*** Mega operations per second (MTOPS).

Quality Marks

In October 1995, the Ministry of International Trade and Industry (MITI) entered into an agreement with the U.S. Environmental Protection Agency (EPA) to develop an Energy Star Program for office equipment in Japan. The products concerned are personal computers, displays, printers, facsimile and copying machines, scanners, and multi-function devices. The agreement sets forth a specific plan for MITI and EPA to co-ordinate their programme activities to maximise the energy savings from office equipment. The Japanese and U.S. programmes maintain identical product specifications, and manufacturers which join one country's programme enjoy privileges in the other country's programme.

NEW ZEALAND

Information Labels

New Zealand has one indigenous energy efficiency label for household appliances — the Electrical Development Association's scheme for labelling electric storage water heaters. However, Australian appliance labels are recognised to some degree, as product suppliers with interests on both sides of the Tasman Sea often display Australian labels on their products sold in New Zealand. In 1988, New Zealand adopted the Australian energy label for refrigerators, dishwashers, clothes washers, clothes dryers, and room air conditioners on a voluntary basis (Cogan 1994). The labelling scheme is endorsed by the government, but run and managed by a third party. There have been proposals to make an Australian-style label mandatory, but the proposals have not been approved by the government.

The Energy Efficiency and Conservation Authority (EECA), the organisation in charge of New Zealand's efforts to improve energy efficiency, has worked on resolving technical development issues related to labelling, test methods and harmonisation with Australia. It has taken part in the deliberations of the joint standards committees working on energy labelling of appliances, and has also developed a draft labelling code of practice and compliance mechanisms which would be used to underpin future appliance labelling registration and mutual recognition with Australia (EECA 1995) (Cogan, 1997).

Standards

New Zealand has a standard specifying minimum energy efficiency requirements for heat loss from domestic-type hot water systems. It applies to both electric and gas hot water cylinders. The standard also reflects changes in energy efficiency installation practices and gives methods to meet minimum acceptable levels. Information is given on acceptable maximum pipe lengths, pipe insulation materials, and minimum thermal insulation of vent, pressure relief and distribution pipes (Cogan, 1997).

EECA has been active in the joint Australia and New Zealand standards committees working on minimum energy performance standards for refrigerators and electric storage water heaters. The organisation has also worked on a domestic minimum energy performance standards programme for a variety of residential appliances — including adoption of the Australian refrigerator standards — and industrial and commercial equipment — initially industrial motors and fluorescent lamps and ballasts (Cogan, 1997) No such standards have as yet been implemented.

NORWAY

Norway has implemented energy labelling for clothes (tumble) dryers, clothes washers, dishwashers, lamps, and refrigerators following the European Union directives on this matter (IEA, 1999).

SWITZERLAND

In the 1990s, Switzerland used a system of target values with supporting endorsement labels to improve the energy efficiency of household appliances and the standby power use of home and office electronics equipment. The programme is currently being revised.

Target Values and Endorsement Labels	household appliances — clothes dryers, clothes washers, dishwashers, ovens, refrigerators, and freezers electronics equipment — fax machines, monitors, personal computers, photocopiers, printers, televisions, videocassette recorders

Energy matters in Switzerland have traditionally been the responsibility of the cantons and municipalities. It was only in a referendum held in September 1990 that the Swiss adopted a constitutional amendment authorising the Federal Government to carry out a national energy policy in pursuit of specific goals, such as energy efficiency and an economic and environmentally benign energy supply. The "Energy 2000" Action Programme, launched in 1991 in response to the referendum, sets out energy efficiency policy initiatives and other measures intended to stabilise Switzerland's fossil fuel consumption and CO_2 emissions at their 1990 levels by 2000 (IEA 1994). One of the legislative initiatives in Energy 2000 led to the adoption of the Decree on the Use of Energy (DEU) by the Swiss Federal Parliament. The DEU, which became effective in March 1992, gave the Swiss Federal Office of Energy the power to issue requirements concerning the energy consumption of electrical appliances. Parliamentarians stated that mandatory energy efficiency standards should not be introduced unless the energy consumption appliances on the market failed to attain certain goals (target values) issued by the government for set dates in the future. However, should the target value approach fail, mandatory standards could be imposed without seeking further political approval.

Targets

The target values were intended to send clear signals to manufacturers to accelerate the development of energy-efficient household appliances and office and entertainment electronics equipment. Manufacturers were asked to reduce the energy consumption of their products to specified levels by given deadlines. The target values and deadlines were fixed in collaboration with the manufacturers.

The intention was the after the deadline 80-95 per cent of the devices sold, depending on the type of equipment, should use less energy than the target values. The target value system did not set a standard which all models must satisfy but rather a target which applied to the average of the entire new sales weighted stock. This meant that models less efficient than the target value could continue to be sold provided that the average of the new stock satisfied the target.

Energy consumption target values were set for all major household appliances, including refrigerators (1 January 1994), electric ovens (1 June 1994), dishwashers (1 June 1994), washing machines (1 June 1994) and tumble dryers (1 June 1994). The voluntary target agreements were negotiated with the same manufacturers that produce and supply refrigerators within the European Union. All the refrigerators found on the Swiss market are also sold on the European Union market though not necessarily vice versa. The Swiss efficiency categories did not make allowances for frost-free refrigerators and group the 0-, 1-, 2- and 3-star models into the same efficiency category.

Target values were also been set for standby power use of computers, monitors and terminals, printers, copiers, facsimile machines and home entertainment electronics, including televisions and video cassette recorders.

The evaluation process of the target value system was very complex so there was always a lag involved in understanding the state of the market. The Swiss authorities tracked all the models sold on the market to understand if the average of the entire new sales-weighted stock met the targets.

Quality Marks

The target value programme was complemented by the E2000 an endorsement label, which indicated models' energy consumption relative to a measure of progress towards the target. In 1999, Switzerland abandoned this label and adopted the Group for Efficient Appliances label.

TURKEY

Turkey has not yet implemented labels and standards for appliances and equipment, but has a number of measures under consideration. A Working Group chaired by the National Energy Conservation Center (NECC) on the efficiency of household appliances and air-conditioners has been set up with participation from the private sector and public organisations concerned. Energy efficiency standards and regulations are in preparation for outdoor (street) lighting. Studies on the regulation of labelling for major domestic appliances have just been initiated by a sub-group that includes the representatives from General Directorate of Electrical Power Resources Survey and Development Administration (EIE), the Turkish Standards Institute, the Ministry of Industry and Trade and the Under-Secretary of Foreign Trade (IEA, 1999).

UNITED STATES

The United States makes extensive use of information labels, quality marks and standards to improve the energy efficiency of appliances and equipment. As of June 2000, fourteen appliances are required to carry energy information labels, and twenty-five products are required to meet minimum energy efficiency standards. In addition, endorsement labels (Energy Star) are used for home and office electronic equipment, buildings and a variety of household products.

Comparison Labels and Standards	clothes washers; central air conditioners; dishwashers; fluorescent lamps and ballasts; compact fluorescent lamps; freezers; furnaces; general service incandescent lamps; instantaneous water heaters; heat pump water heaters; refrigerators; room air conditioners; swimming pool heaters; and water heaters
Standards only	central air conditioners heat pumps; clothes dryers; commercial furnaces and boilers; commercial packaged air conditioners and heat pumps; commercial water heaters; direct-fired space heaters; electric motors (1-200 hp); boilers; kitchen ranges and ovens
Endorsement Labels	domestic appliances, heating and cooling equipment, home electronics, office equipment, lighting fixtures and bulbs, windows and buildings

The authority for nearly all U.S. federal-level energy efficiency testing, labelling and standards programmes comes from the laws outlined in Box A1.1.

Box A1.1   Principal U.S. Federal Labelling and Standards Laws
and Procedural Guidelines

Energy Policy and Conservation Act, 1975 (EPCA)

■ Directed the National Institute of Standards and Technology (NIST) to develop standard test procedures for measuring the energy efficiency of appliances.

■ Directed the Federal Trade Commission (FTC) to develop and promulgate information labels listing energy use for new appliances.

■ Directed the Department of Energy (DOE) to develop voluntary appliance efficiency targets.

National Energy Conservation Policy Act, 1978 (NECPA)

■ Directed DOE to set mandatory standards in replacement of the EPCA voluntary targets.

■ Gave federal standards pre-emption over state standards.

National Appliance Energy Conservation Act of 1987 and amendments of 1988 (NAECA).

■ Established, in the law itself, standards for the twelve categories of appliances covered under EPCA and NECPA.

■ Instructed DOE to set standards on one additional product if technically feasible and economically justified.

■ Required DOE to review and update the standards to keep pace with technological improvements.

■ Strengthened the pre-emption of federal standards over state standards.

Energy Policy Act of 1992 (EPAct)

- Directed DOE to support voluntary national testing and information programmes for widely used types of office equipment.

- Established, in the law itself, energy standards for nine categories of energy-using and water-using commercial sector products, electric motors, lighting products, plumbing products and office equipment.

- Instructed DOE to set standards on three additional products if technically feasible and economically justified.

Procedures, Interpretations and Policies for Consideration of New or Revised Energy Conservation Standards for Consumer Products, 1996.

- Describes the process that will be used to consider new or revised energy efficiency standards and lists a number of factors and analyses that will be considered at specified points in the process. These procedures are intended to supplement, rather than supplant, the statutory criteria in the laws above.

Information Labels

Mandatory energy labelling of appliances and equipment was authorised by the Energy Policy and Conservation Act (EPCA) in 1975, and the ensuing Energy-Guide programme took effect in May 1980. The Federal Trade Commission (FTC) developed and manages this programme. The initial Energy-Guide rules required labels on seven types of electricity, gas, oil and propane using appliances: refrigerators, freezers, dishwashers, water heaters, room air conditioners, clothes washers and most furnaces. Since then, additional energy-using products have been regulated, and water-use labels have become mandatory on showerheads, faucets, water closets (toilets) and urinals.

Until late 1994, the labels focused primarily on energy costs, denominated in dollars. The labels showed the model's estimated annual energy cost and the range of energy costs of similar models (based on national average energy prices). They also showed the energy costs that could be expected under various energy rates, for example 2, 4, 6, 8, 10 and 12 cents/kWh of electricity. In 1994, the labels were revised to improve their readability and usefulness to consumers. Though the new labels still indicate the estimated annual energy cost, they emphasise energy use in physical units (kilowatt-hours of electricity, therms of gas, gallons of oil or propane) or energy efficiency ratios.[34] They show the (1) model's annual energy use or energy efficiency ratio, (2) the comparative range of these values for all similar models and (3) the model's estimated yearly energy cost, calculated at the national average energy rate. Energy efficiency ratios are used for climate-control appliances, for which energy consumption varies by region and seasons. The annual cost appears on the label in the case of room air conditioners, and on fact sheets and in industry-produced product directories for the other climate-control appliances.

Quality Marks

At least two quality marks — Green Seal and Energy Star — exist in the United States to designate efficient appliances and equipment.

Green Seal is a non-profit, environmental labelling and consumer education organisation that certifies products that are designed and manufactured in an environmentally responsible manner. Once standards are established, manufacturers can apply for an evaluation

---

34. There are various product-specific energy efficiency ratios: annual fuel utilisation efficiency (AFUE) for furnaces, energy efficiency ratio (EER) for room air conditioners, seasonal energy efficiency ratio (SEER) for the cooling function of central air conditioners and heat pumps, heating seasonal performance factor (HSPF) for the heating function of heat pumps, and thermal efficiency (TE) for swimming pool heaters.

of their products; those that comply can use the Green Seal Certification mark on their products and in their advertising. Certification standards have been established for refrigerators, freezers, clothes washers, clothes dryers, dishwashers, and stoves and ovens.

Energy Star is a voluntary partnership of the Department of Energy (DOE), the Environmental Protection Agency (EPA), product manufacturers, distributors, utilities, energy-efficiency advocates, consumers, and other organisations. The programme, begun in 1992, combines product labelling with information and promotion campaigns and alternative financing activities.

Product labels. EPA and DOE work with manufacturers and other interested parties to establish energy-efficiency specifications for existing, proven technologies. Product models that exceed these specifications can be identified with the Energy Star label. For products subject to minimum efficiency standards, the models qualify for the Energy Star label if they exceed the standards by a certain amount, varying from product to product. Typically, the top quartile of models within a product class qualify for Energy Star. Other products, such as office equipment, the models qualify for the label if they have special features which enable them to use less energy than similar products.

Objective information. The programme provides non-technical fact sheets, brochures, and interactive websites to help consumers better understand the economic and environmental benefits of using energy-efficient products. This information also gives consumers a way to verify manufacturers' efficiency claims for their products. One project, the Purchasing Initiative, helps organisations purchase energy-efficient products by assisting them with: developing life cycle cost analyses, preparing bids, specifying particular brands, educating employees about new policies, gaining recognition about their commitment to the environment and savings, overcoming barriers and discovering benefits of energy-efficient purchasing.

Energy efficiency promotion. The programme works actively with national, regional and local groups, including energy-efficiency advocacy groups, utilities, retailers and others, to not only promote awareness of the Energy Star programme and label, but also to ensure that the message reflects local concerns and needs. One of the promotion activities is mass-media advertising,

Alternative financing. The programme works with financial institutions to help them to develop and market alternative financing for Energy Star products in order to reduce the costs of owning energy-efficient equipment and products (US EPA, 1998).

As of November 1999, more than 500 manufacturers are offering over 13 000 product models that qualify for the Energy Star label. In addition, more than 200 builders and developers have committed to build over 15 000 Energy Star homes. The products include domestic appliances, heating and cooling equipment, home electronics, office equipment, lighting fixtures and bulbs, windows and buildings. The programme was given a major boost in April 1993 when President Clinton signed an Executive Order requiring all federal government agencies to purchase Energy Star computers, monitors, and printers where commercially available. This market-pull strategy involving the world's largest purchaser of office equipment, the U.S. government, had a strong effect on the market penetration of Energy Star equipment, and was one of the primary drivers leading to the programme's success.

There is also an international element to the programme, involving joint energy efficiency specifications and a common logo. Participating countries offer mutual recognition to compliant products, such that Energy Star labels affixed to products in one country are valid in the other country(ies) as well. So far, the United States, Japan and Australia participate in the International Energy

Star programme. Discussions concerning participation of the European Union are ongoing. The products included in the programme are personal computers, displays, printers, and facsimile and copying machines.

Standards — State-Federal; Voluntary-Mandatory; Negotiated[35]

The establishment of appliance standards in the United States took many years, and involved many organisations and numerous actions — some consensual, some confrontational — at both the federal and state levels. In brief, federal appliance efficiency standards were first authorised in a voluntary form in 1975 and then made mandatory in 1978. However, it was not until 1988 that efficiency standards for most major types of residential energy equipment were established, and the 1990s that they came into effect.[36] Apart from a temporary moratorium during 1995-96, the standards have been, and continue to be, updated and strengthened regularly.

Efficiency standards were first proposed in the United States in the 1970s, before the first oil shock. The earliest concrete proposals were made California and the states in the northeast, as they confronted regional issues concerning the reliability of the electricity system and the environmental impacts of power plant siting. In 1974, the California Energy Commission was established and given the authority to set appliance efficiency standards.

The following year, as part of its response to the oil shock, the federal government adopted the Energy Policy and Conservation Act (EPCA), which among other things called for the Federal Energy

---

35. This section draws heavily from Nadel, 1996.

36. The first federal standards of any consequence — on refrigerators, freezers, room air conditioners and water heaters — took effect on 1 January 1990. Some minor standards for clothes washers, clothes dryers, and dishwashers took effect on 1 January 1988. The requirements were: no pilot lights for gas clothes dryers, availability of a cold rinse option for clothes washers, and availability of an option to dry without heat for dishwashers. Most models of these products already satisfied these standards when NAECA was written.

Administration, predecessor to the DOE, to develop voluntary efficiency targets for appliances.

Then in 1975-77, California and several other states adopted mandatory energy efficiency standards. This prompted the Carter Administration to propose converting DOE's voluntary targets to mandatory standards. Manufacturers were opposed to mandatory standards generally, but were particularly concerned about multiple state standards. To address this concern, the resulting National Energy Conservation Policy Act (NECPA) gave DOE standards pre-emptive power over state standards. The law also instructed DOE to assess whether the proposed standards were "economically justifiable," including consideration of their impact on manufacturers. DOE proposed standards for a number of appliances, but failed to issue final rules before the Carter Administration left office in early 1981. The following Reagan Administration opposed standards on ideological grounds, and requested that Congress de-authorise them. When Congress refused, the Administration sought to delay and circumvent substantive standards through administrative means. These actions were challenged successfully in court by the Natural Resources Defense Council (NRDC), an environmental advocacy organisation.

In the meantime, many states had become concerned about the lack of progress on appliance efficiency. The California Energy Commission issued standards on refrigerators and central air conditioners in 1984, and by 1986 five other states had adopted standards on one or more products.

Given the momentum of state standard setting actions and the court ruling in favour of the NRDC, directing the DOE to develop substantive standards, home appliance manufacturers offered to negotiate new federal legislation that would effectively trade off national standards for increased pre-emption of state efforts. The negotiations involved the NRDC — working with the state energy offices, the American Council for an Energy-Efficient Economy (ACEEE) and other environmental and consumer organisations — and the appliance manufacturers, along with interested parties such as utilities (gas and electric; municipal and investor owned), retailers, home builders, mobile home producers, etc. Notably, the DOE did not participate in the negotiations, except to contribute analysis on the costs and benefits of standards for eight types of appliances mandated by NECPA. The negotiations led to an agreement proposing specific initial standard levels and implementation dates. Manufacturers supported it because it provided a single national standard which pre-empted most of the multiple state and local standards that were in effect. Energy efficiency advocates endorsed it because it provided national standards as well as the likelihood that the DOE would set more stringent standards. The agreement was very attractive to Congress because of the broad and virtually unanimous stakeholder support. The resulting legislation, the National Appliance Energy Conservation Act of 1987 (NAECA) passed Congress, was signed by President Reagan and became law on 17 March 1987. The nature of the negotiations resulted in the technical details of the energy efficiency regulations being written directly into the law. The agreement led stakeholders to seek further consensual legislation, resulting in the NAECA Amendments of 1988 which replaced ballast standards in effect in several states with national standards at the same level. NAECA, as amended, designates minimum efficiency or maximum energy consumption levels for thirteen categories of covered products and requires DOE to update and strengthen these standards on a regular basis in order to keep pace with technological improvements.

The theme for initiating national standards at the state level had been set. Massachusetts passed legislation requiring its energy office to set standards for fluorescent and incandescent lamps. The prospect of additional state regulations set the stage for new negotiations on national standards. The negotiations were coupled with similar discussions on water efficiency. The negotiations, covering six energy-using products and three water-using products were incorporated into the efficiency provisions of the national Energy Policy Act of 1992 (EPAct). Enactment of EPAct expanded the U.S. standards programme into the equipment used by commercial and industrial facilities.

Standards — Process for Revisions and Updates

The nature of the NAECA and EPAct standards, being based on stakeholder agreements, gives the U.S. standards programme a solid, unambiguous, consensus-based foundation. This is evident in that the technical details of initial standards are written into the law itself. However, the programme has not been without controversy. The programme encountered serious organisational, budgetary and analytical problems in reviewing and updating of standards in the early 1990s. The situation came to a head in 1995, when a Congress with an anti-regulatory sentiment took office. Manufacturers expressed grave concerns about the programme, and asked Congress to intervene. As part of its 1996 budgetary process, Congress issued a one-year moratorium on proposing or issuing energy conservation standards. DOE recognised the problem earlier, and even before the moratorium, had begun making changes to the rulemaking process. Then in September 1995, it launched a high-profile, public process improvement activity to restore confidence in the programme. The process improvement exercise involved many stakeholders, manufacturers and environmental public interest groups, deliberating issues of planning, input and analysis and decision making. New process rules, entitled *Procedures, Interpretations and Policies for Consideration of New or Revised Energy Conservation Standards for Consumer Products*, drafted in consultation with the stakeholders, were published in July 1996 (Federal Register, 61FR3694). The major objectives of the new rules fall into three categories:

Procedural — provide for early input from stakeholders; increase the predictability of the rulemaking timetable; reduce the time and cost of developing standards.

Analytical — increase the use of outside expertise; eliminate design options early in the process; conduct thorough analyses of impacts; use transparent and robust analytical methods.

Interpretive — fully consider non-regulatory approaches; articulate policies to guide the selection of standards; support efforts to build consensus on standards (Miller, 1997).

Central to the new process is the consultation with stakeholders at all stages. Stakeholders now participate in the development of market analyses and technology characterisation, the screening of design options, the engineering analysis (using a conventional design-approach or cost-efficiency curves), the life-cycle cost analysis, the national benefit analysis and the analyses of impacts on manufacturers, consumers, utilities and the environment. The impact analyses now focus on ranges, rather than averages. Moreover, the DOE created an advisory committee to guarantee stakeholders access to the process and the continuing process evaluation and improvement.

NORTH AMERICAN CO-ORDINATION — NAFTA

Canada and the United States have been quite active in the area of harmonisation. Many of the efficiency standard levels are the same as well as many of the test procedures. More recently, partially as a result of the North American Free Trade Agreement (NAFTA), Canada, Mexico and the United States have entered into negotiations to harmonise test protocols for certain appliances. This may lead to greater harmonisation of labels and standards requirements also. At this time there are no official agreements between the countries. The Canada, Mexico and the United States already use the same test procedure for refrigerators, room air conditioners and motors. Mexico is not yet testing the appliances though.

PACIFIC RIM CO-ORDINATION — APEC

There are currently investigations under way within Asia Pacific Economic Cooperation (APEC), of which Australia, Canada, Japan, New Zealand and the United States are members, to assess the feasibility of mutual recognition of laboratories and harmonising test protocols, labelling and efficiency standards. This is being undertaken by the Energy Working Group of APEC, Energy Efficiency and Conservation Experts Group.

APPENDIX B
PRINCIPLES FOR THE CONDUCT OF ENGINEERING AND MARKET ANALYSES IN THE U.S. STANDARDS PROGRAMME

In the United States, the law authorising standards and its accompanying procedural rules set out explicit guidelines for the conduct of engineering and market analyses. The principles upon which the engineering, manufacturer impact and consumer impact analyses are based are described below (*italics added*) (US DOE, 1996).

Notably, in the introductory notes to the rules, the US DOE acknowledges that using ever more elaborate quantitative approaches carries the risk of unacceptable delays and incomprehensible analysis and results. For these reasons, the Department will seek to balance appropriately the use of quantitative and qualitative approaches, with the goal of providing the most useful information upon which to make the required judgments.

PRINCIPLES FOR THE CONDUCT OF ENGINEERING ANALYSIS

The Department will use the most appropriate means available to determine the *efficiency/cost relationship* (of the subject product), including an overall system approach or engineering modelling to predict the improvement in efficiency that can be expected from individual design options.[37] From this efficiency/cost relationship,

---

37. *Design options refer to alternative component technologies and configurations for the products in question.*

measures such as *payback, life cycle cost, and energy savings* can be developed. The Department, *in consultation with interested parties*, will *identify issues that will be examined* in the engineering analysis.

The engineering analysis begins with the list of design options developed in consultation with the interested parties as a result of the screening process. In consultation with the *technology/industry expert peer review group*, the Department will establish the likely cost and performance improvement of each design option. *Ranges and uncertainties of cost and performance* will be established, although efforts will be made to minimize uncertainties by using measures such as test data or component or material supplier information where available. Estimated uncertainties will be carried forward in subsequent analyses. The use of quantitative models will be supplemented by qualitative assessments as appropriate.

The next step includes *identifying, modifying or developing* any *engineering models* necessary to predict the efficiency impact of any one or combination of design options on the product. A base case configuration or starting point will be established as well as the order and combination/blending of the design options to be evaluated. The DOE, utilizing expert consultants, will then perform the engineering analysis and develop the *cost efficiency curve* for the product. The cost efficiency curve and any necessary models will be subject to peer review before being issued (as a formal part of the regulatory dossier).

PRINCIPLES FOR THE ANALYSIS OF IMPACTS ON MANUFACTURERS

The Department will analyse the impact of standards on manufacturers with substantial input from manufacturers and other interested parties. The use of quantitative models will be supplemented by qualitative assessments by industry experts.

Issue identification The Department, in consultation with interested parties, will identify issues that will require greater consideration in the detailed manufacturer impact analysis. Possible issues may include identification of specific types or groups of manufacturers and concerns over access to technology.

Industry Characterisation

Prior to initiating detailed impact studies, the Department will seek input on the present and past industry structure and market characteristics, such as: (1) manufacturers and their relative market shares; (2) manufacturer characteristics, such as whether manufacturers make a full line of models or serve a niche market; (3) trends in the number of manufacturers; (4) financial situation of manufacturers; (5) trends in product characteristics and retail markets; and (6) identification of other relevant regulatory actions and a description of the nature and timing of any likely impacts.

Cost Impacts on Manufacturers

The costs of labour, material, engineering, tooling, and capital are difficult to estimate, manufacturer-specific, and usually proprietary. The Department will seek input from interested parties on the treatment of cost issues. Manufacturers will be encouraged to offer suggestions as to possible sources of data and appropriate data collection methodologies. Costing issues to be addressed include: (1) estimates of total cost impacts, including product-specific costs (based on cost impacts estimated for the engineering analysis) and front-end investment/conversion costs for the full range of product models; (2) range of uncertainties in estimates of average cost, considering alternative designs and technologies which may vary cost impacts and changes in costs of material, labour and other inputs which may vary costs; and (3) variable cost impacts on particular types of manufacturers, considering factors such as atypical sunk costs or characteristics of specific models which may increase or decrease costs.

Impacts on product sales, features, prices and cost recovery. In order to
make manufacturer cash flow calculations, it is necessary to predict
the number of products sold and their sale price. This requires an
assessment of the likely impacts of price changes on the number of
products sold and on typical features of models sold. Past analyses
have relied on price and shipment data generated by economic
models. The Department will develop additional estimates of prices
and shipments by drawing on multiple sources of data and
experience including: actual shipment and pricing experience, data
from manufacturers, retailers and other market experts, financial
models, and sensitivity analyses. The possible impacts of candidate
standard levels on consumer choices among competing fuels will be
explicitly considered where relevant.

Measures of Impact

The manufacturer impact analysis will estimate the impacts of
candidate standard levels on the net cash flow of manufacturers.
Computations will be performed for the industry as a whole and for
typical and atypical manufacturers. ... Impacts to be analysed include:
(1) industry net present value, with sensitivity analyses based on
uncertainty of costs, sales prices and sales volumes; (2) cash flows,
by year; and (3) other measures of impact, such as revenue, net
income and return on equity, as appropriate. The characteristics of
atypical manufacturers worthy of special consideration will be
determined in consultation with manufacturers and other interested
parties and may include: manufacturers incurring higher or lower
than average costs; and manufacturers experiencing greater or fewer
adverse impacts on sales. Alternative scenarios based on other
methods of estimating cost or sales impacts also will be performed,
as needed.

Cumulative Impacts of other Federal Regulatory Actions

(1) The Department will recognize and seek to mitigate the overlapping effects on manufacturers of new or revised DOE standards and other regulatory actions affecting the same products. DOE will analyse and consider the impact on manufacturers of multiple product-specific regulatory actions. These factors will be considered in setting rulemaking priorities, assessing manufacturer impacts of a particular standard, and establishing the effective date for a new or revised standard. In particular, DOE will seek to propose effective dates for new or revised standards that are appropriately coordinated with other regulatory actions to mitigate any cumulative burden. (2) If the Department determines that a proposed standard would impose a significant impact on product manufacturers within three years of the effective date of another DOE standard that imposes significant impacts on the same manufacturers (or divisions thereof, as appropriate), the Department will, in addition to evaluating the impact on manufacturers of the proposed standard, assess the joint impacts of both standards on manufacturers. (3) If the Department is directed to establish or revise standards for products that are components of other products subject to standards, the Department will consider the interaction between such standards in setting rulemaking priorities and assessing manufacturer impacts of a particular standard. The Department will assess, as part of the engineering and impact analyses, the cost of components subject to efficiency standards.

Summary of Quantitative and Qualitative Assessments

The summary of quantitative and qualitative assessments will contain a description and discussion of uncertainties. Alternative estimates of impacts, resulting from the different potential scenarios developed throughout the analysis, will be explicitly presented in the final analysis results.

Key modelling and analytical tools In its assessment of the likely impacts of standards on manufacturers, the Department will use models which are clear and understandable, feature accessible calculations, and have assumptions that are clearly explained. As a starting point, the Department will use the Government Regulatory Impact Model (GRIM).

PRINCIPLES FOR THE ANALYSIS OF IMPACTS ON CONSUMERS[38]

Early Consideration of Impacts on Consumer Utility

The Department will consider at the earliest stages of the development of a standard whether particular design options will lessen the utility of the covered products to the consumer.

Impacts on Product Availability

The Department will determine, ... whether a proposed standard is likely to result in the unavailability of any covered product type with performance characteristics (including reliability), features, sizes, capacities, and volumes that are substantially the same as products generally available in the U.S. at the time.

Department of Justice Review

As required by law, the Department will solicit the views of the Justice Department on any lessening of competition that is likely to result from the imposition of a proposed standard and will give the views provided full consideration in assessing economic justification of a proposed standard.

---

38. In the introductory notes to the rules, DOE states that "consumers have rarely participated directly in standards development. In order to address concerns about the lack of such direct participation, DOE will seek to strengthen its efforts to inform and involve consumers and consumer representatives in the process of developing standards."

Variation in consumer impacts The Department will use regional analysis and sensitivity analysis tools, as appropriate, to evaluate the potential distribution of impacts of candidate standards levels among different subgroups of consumers. The Department will consider impacts on significant segments of consumers in determining standards levels. Where there are significant negative impacts on identifiable subgroups, DOE will consider the efficacy of voluntary approaches as a means to achieve potential energy savings.

Payback Period and First Cost

(1) In the assessment of consumer impacts of standards, the Department will consider Life-Cycle Cost, Payback Period and Cost of Conserved Energy to evaluate the savings in operating expenses relative to increases in purchase price.[39] The Department intends to increase the level of sensitivity analysis and scenario analysis for future rulemakings. The results of these analyses will be carried throughout the analysis and the ensuing uncertainty described. (2) If, in the analysis of consumer impacts, the Department determines that a candidate standard level would result in a substantial increase in the product first costs to consumers or would not pay back such additional first costs through energy cost savings in less than three years, Department will specifically assess the likely impacts of such a standard on low-income households, product sales and fuel switching.

---

39. In the introductory notes to the rules, DOE states its expectation "that the use of these methods will result in more economically efficient standards than reliance on pay-back period alone, while achieving the similar result of avoiding negative impacts to identifiable population groups."

REFERENCES AND BIBLIOGRAPHY

CITED REFERENCES

AGO (2000), Australian Greenhouse Office, National Appliance and Equipment Energy Efficiency Program, *Projected Combined Impacts from an Extended and Enhanced Program*, March 2000. (www.greenhouse.gov.au/energyefficiency)

APEC (1994), Asia-Pacific Economic Cooperation, *Compendium of Energy Efficiency and Conservation Policies/Programs, Regulations and Standards in the Asia-Pacific Economic Cooperation (APEC) Member Economies*, 1994.

Appliance Efficiency (1999), Newsletter of IDEA, the International Network for Domestic Energy-Efficient Appliances, volume 3, issue 4, 1999.

Appliance Efficiency (2000), Newsletter of IDEA, the International Network for Domestic Energy-Efficient Appliances, volume 4, issue 1, 2000.

BERTOLDI, P. (1997), "European Union Efforts to Promote More Efficient Appliances," *Energy Efficiency in Household Appliances*, 10-12 November 1997, Florence, Italy, ed. Bertoldi, Ricci and Huenges Wajer, (Springer, Berlin) 1999.

BERTOLDI, P. (1999), "Energy Efficient Equipment within SAVE: Activities, Strategies, Success and Barriers," *Proceedings of the SAVE Conference for an Energy Efficient Millenium*, Graz, Austria, 8-10 November 1999. (www.eva.wsr.ac.at/save-conf/programmes.htm)

BREITENBERG, M.A. (1997), National Institute of Standards and Technology, Office of Standards Services, *The ABC's of the U.S. Conformity Assessment System*, NISTIR 6014, April 1997.

CADDET (1997), IEA/OECD Centre for the Analysis and Dissemination of Demonstrated Energy Technologies, Energy Efficiency, *Saving Energy With Appliance Labelling*, Maxi Brochure 09, (Sittard, The Netherlands) 1997.

COGAN, D. (1994), "Refrigerator and Freezer Energy Efficiency Labelling in Australia and New Zealand", Energy Efficiency and Conservation Authority, Wellington, NZ, 1994.

COGAN, D. (1997), "The Backroom Work Behind the Backbone of Energy Efficiency," *Energy-Wise News*, Issue 3, June/July 1997.

CUSHMAN, J. H. (1995), "GM Agrees to Ante Up $45 Million in Big Recall," *The New York Times*, 1 December 1995, cited in Meier, 1998.

DAŠEK, M. (1999), "Introduction and Implementation of Legislation Concerning the Energy Efficiency Labelling and Standardisation of Domestic Appliances in CEE Countries," *Proceedings of the SAVE Conference for an Energy Efficient Millenium*, Graz, Austria, 8-10 November 1999. (www.eva.wsr.ac.at/save-conf/programmes.htm)

DES ROSIERS, J.-P. (1997) and J. Cockburn, "Regulating Appliance Energy Efficiency in Canada: Some Similarities and Differences with the US," *Energy and Buildings*, 26 (1) 1997, pp. 89-94.

EECA (1995), Energy Efficiency and Conservation Authority, *Annual Report 1994/95 and Business Plan 1995/96*, Wellington, New Zealand.

EMR (1994), Canadian Department of Energy, Mines and Resources, "Regulatory Impact Analysis Statement" in *Canada Gazette Part 1*, March 19, 1994, pp. 1715-1726. (cited in Turiel 1995).

ENGLERYD, A. (1998), S. Attali, P. Menanteau, H. Lefebvre, E. de Almeida, L. Pagliano, P. Corkish, C. Lopes, H. Ritter, K. Ostertag, M. Landwehr, H. Härkönen, R. Trines, M. Klootwijk, A. Persson, H. Nilsson, S. Thomas and G. Wohlauf, *Procurement for Market Transformation for Energy-Efficient Products*, for the Commission of the European Community SAVE Program, 1998.

EWWE (1997), "Industry Sectors in EU Agreement to Cut Products' Energy Consumption," *Environment Watch: Western Europe*, 17 October 1997.

GEA (Group for Efficient Appliances) (1993), "Study on Energy Efficiency Standards for Domestic Refrigeration Appliances" CEC-DG XVII, ADEME, DEA, NOVEM.

GELLER, H. (1997), "National Appliance Efficiency Standards in the USA: Cost-Effective Federal Regulations," *Energy and Buildings*, 26 (1) 1997, pp. 101-109.

GELLER-GOLDSTEIN SZILARD LECTURE (1999), *Physics and Society*, v. 28, no. 2, (American Physical Society, College Park, Maryland, USA, 1999), cited in Rosenfeld, A.H. and D.A. Bassett, Office of Energy Efficiency and Renewable Energy, U.S. Department of Energy, *The Dependence of Annual Energy Efficiency Improvement (AEEI) on Price and Policy*, presented at The IEA International Workshop on Technologies to Reduce Greenhouse Gas Emissions: Engineering-Economic Analyses of Conserved Energy and Carbon, Washington, D.C., 5-7 May 1999 (http://www.iea.org/workshop/engecon).

GREENING, L.A. (1996), A. Sanstad, J.E. McMahon, T. Wenzel, S.J. Pickle, "Retrospective Analysis of National Energy Efficiency Standards for Refrigerators," *Proceedings of the 1996 ACEEE Summer Study*, 1996.

GWA (1991), George Wilkenfeld and Associates, Residential Appliances in Australia: An Assessment of Market and Technology Developments, with Particular Reference to Energy-Efficiency, prepared for the State Electricity Commission of Victoria, June 1991.

GWA (1993), George Wilkenfeld and Associates, with Lawrence Berkeley National Laboratory, *Benefits and Costs of Implementing Minimum Energy Performance Standards for Household Electrical Appliances in Australia*. prepared for the State Electricity Commission of Victoria, July 1993.

HARRINGTON, L. (1994), "Appliance Energy Efficiency in Australia," presented to Energy Efficiency Business Week, Prague Czech Republic, 8-10 November 1994.

HARRINGTON, L. (1997), and G. Wilkenfeld, "Appliance Efficiency Programs in Australia: Labelling and Standards," *Energy and Buildings*, 26 (1) 1997 pp. 81-88.

IEA (1989), International Energy Agency, *Electricity End-Use Efficiency*, OECD, Paris, 1989

IEA (1994), International Energy Agency, *Energy Policies of IEA Countries 1994 Review*, OECD, Paris, 1994.

IEA (1997), International Energy Agency, Danish Energy Agency and Energy Charter, *Energy Efficiency Initiative*, OECD, Paris, 1997.

IEA (1999), International Energy Agency, *Energy Efficiency Update*, No. 22, May 1999. (http://www.iea.org/pubs/newslett/eneeff/table.htm)

ISO (1991), International Organization for Standardization, *General Terms and their Definitions Concerning Standardization and Related Activities*, ISO/IEC Guide 2, 1991.

IWAMOTO, K. (1992), "Energy Efficiency Standards in Japan," *Proceedings, International Energy Conference on Use of Efficiency Standards in Energy Policy*, Sophia-Antipolis, France, 4-5 June 1992, IEA/OECD, Paris.

KOOMEY, J.G. (1998), S.A. Mahler, C.A. Webber and J.E. McMahon, *Projected Regional Impacts of Appliance Efficiency Standards for the U.S. Residential Sector*, Report LBNL-39511, Energy Analysis Program, Energy and Environment Division, Ernest Orlando Lawrence Berkeley National Laboratory, February 1998, see also *Energy The International Journal* v.24, n.1 January 1999.

LAPONCHE, B. (1997), B. Jamet, M. Colombier and S. Attali, *Energy Efficiency for a Sustainable World*, International Conseil Énergie (ICE), Paris, 1997.

LBNL (1995), Lawrence Berkeley National Laboratory, U.S. Department of Energy, *From the Lab to the Marketplace: Making America's Buildings More Energy Efficient*, March 1995 (http://eetd.lbl.gov/cbs/Lab2Mkt/Lab2Mkt.html).

MEIER, A.K. (1997a), "Observed Energy Savings from Appliance Efficiency Standards," *Energy and Buildings*, 26 (1) 1997, pp. 111-117.

MEIER, A.K. (1997b) and J.E. Hill, "Energy Test Procedures for Appliances," *Energy and Buildings*, 26 (1) 1997, pp. 23-33.

MEIER, A.K. (1998), "Energy Test Procedures for the Twenty-First Century," presented at the 1998 Appliance Manufacturer Conference & Expo, Nashville, TN, 12-16 October 1998, also available as Lawrence Berkeley National Laboratory Report LBNL-41732, May 1998.

MITI (1999), Japanese Ministry of International Trade and Industry communication to the IEA, 1999.

MELI, L. (1997), "The CECED Commitment for Clothes Washers," *Energy Efficiency in Household Appliances*, 10-12 November 1997, Florence, Italy, ed. Bertoldi, Ricci and Huenges Wajer, (Springer, Berlin) 1999.

MELI, L. (1999), "Can Negotiated Agreements Deliver Efficiency? Industry's Point of View," *Proceedings of the SAVE Conference for an Energy Efficient Millenium*, Graz, Austria, 8-10 November 1999 (www.eva.wsr.ac.at/save-conf/programmes.htm).

MILLER, D.E. (1997), "The U.S. Department of Energy's Appliance Energy Efficiency Process Improvement Effort," *Energy Efficiency in Household Appliances*, 10-12 November 1997, Florence, Italy, ed. Bertoldi, Ricci and Huenges Wajer, (Springer, Berlin) 1999.

NADEL, S. (1996) and D. Goldstein, "Appliance and Equipment Efficiency Standards: History, Impacts, Current Status, and Future Directions," *Proceedings of the ACEEE 1996 Summer Study on Energy*

Efficiency Buildings. (American Council for an Energy-Efficient Economy, Washington, D.C.), 1996.

NAEEEC (1999), Australian National Appliance and Equipment Energy Efficiency Committee, *National Appliance & Equipment Energy Efficiency Program*, October 1999.

NAKAGAMI, H. (1997) and B. Litt, Appliance Standards in Japan, *Energy and Buildings*, 26 (1) 1997, pp. 69-79.

NRC (1995), U.S. National Research Council, International Standards, Conformity Assessment, and U.S. Trade Policy Project Committee, *Standards, Conformity Assessment, and Trade: Into the 21st Century*, National Academy Press, 1995.

NRCan (1995), Natural Resources Canada, *Compliance Policy for the Energy Efficiency Act and the Energy Efficiency Regulations* (Ottawa, Ontario), 1995.

NRCan (1996), Natural Resources Canada, *Influencing Energy Use in Canada, Progress Indicators on Initiatives Delivered by Natural Resources Canada* (Ottawa, Ontario), August 1996.

NRCan (1998), Natural Resources Canada, *Improving Energy Use in Canada — Report to Parliament Under the Energy Efficiency Act, 1996-1997* (Ottawa, Ontario) 1998. (oee.nrcan.gc.ca/seec/report97.htm)

NRCan (2000), Natural Resources Canada, *Improving Energy Use in Canada — Report to Parliament Under the Energy Efficiency Act, 1997-1999* (Ottawa, Ontario) 2000

OECD (1994), Public Management (PUMA) Directorate, Occasional Paper 1994, No. 3, *Performance Management in Government: Performance Measurement and Results-Oriented Management*, (OECD, Paris) 1994.

SCHIELLERUP, P. (1999), J. Winward, and B. Boardman, "Cool Labels," *Proceedings of the SAVE Conference for an Energy Efficient Millenium*, Graz, Austria, 8-10 November 1999 (www.eva.wsr.ac.at/save-conf/programmes.htm).

SFOE (1999), Swiss Federal Office of Energy, "Les appareils électriques ne respectent pas encore les valeurs-cibles de consommation," press release, 25 August 1999.

TURIEL, I. (1995), J. Kollar and J. McMahon, Lawrence Berkeley National Laboratory, *Overview of International Energy Efficiency Standards*, prepared for the IEA with support from the Japanese New Energy and Industrial Technology Development Organisation (NEDO), July 1995.

US DOE (1996), U.S. Department of Energy, Energy Conservation Program for Consumer Products: Procedures for Consideration of New or Revised Energy Conservation Standards for Consumer Products, 61FR3694 (July 15, 1996), also 10 CFR Part 430.

US EPA (1998), *ENERGY STAR® and Related Programs 1997, Annual Report*, United States Environmental Protection Agency, Air and Radiation 6202J, Atmospheric Pollution Prevention Division, 430-R-98-002, March 1998.

WAIDE P. (1995) and B. Lebot, Agence de l'Environnement et de la Maîtrise de l'Energie (Ademe), *Refrigerators and Freezers: Market Characteristics, Energy Use, and Standards Harmonisation*, prepared for the IEA with support from the Japanese New Energy and Industrial Technology Development Organisation (NEDO), November 1995.

WAIDE, P. (1997), B. Lebot, M. Hinnells, "Appliance Energy Standards in Europe," *Energy and Buildings*, 26 (1) 1997 pp. 45-67.

WAIDE, P. (1999a), *Monitoring of Energy Efficiency Trends of European Domestic Refrigeration Appliances*, for the Commission of the European Community SAVE Program, January 1999.

WAIDE, P. (1999b), "Market Analysis and Effect of EU Labelling and Standards: The Example of Cold Appliances," *Proceedings of the SAVE Conference for an Energy Efficient Millenium*, Graz, Austria, 8-10 November 1999 (www.eva.wsr.ac.at/save-conf/programmes.htm).

WILKENFELD, G. (1993), *CADDET Energy Efficiency* newsletter, September, 1993.

WILKENFELD, G. (1997), "Evaluating the Impact of the Australian Household Appliance Energy Efficiency Program," *Energy Efficiency in Household Appliances*, 10-12 November 1997, Florence, Italy, ed. Bertoldi, Ricci and Huenges Wajer, (Springer, Berlin) 1999.

WILSON, D. (1989), L. Schipper, S. Tyler and S. Bartlett, Lawrence Berkeley Laboratory, *Policies and Programs for Promoting Energy Conservation in the Residential Sector: Lessons from Five OECD Countries*, Berkeley, CA, 1989.

WINWARD, J. (1998), P. Schiellerup and B. Boardman, Brenda, Environmental Change Unit, University of Oxford, *Cool Labels*, for the Commission of the European Community SAVE Program, September 1998.

GENERAL BIBLIOGRAPHY

Asia-Pacific Economic Cooperation (APEC), APEC Energy Working Group, *Review of Energy Efficiency Test Standards and Regulations in APEC Member Economies*, 1999.

Appliance Efficiency, Newsletter of IDEA, the International Network for Domestic Energy-Efficient Appliances.

Duffy, J., International Institute for Energy Conservation (IIEC), *Energy Labelling, Standards and Building Codes: A Global Survey and Assessment for Selected Developing Countries*, GEEI Publications, Washington, D.C., 1996.

Energy and Buildings, 26 (1) 1997, Special Issue devoted to Energy Efficiency Standards for Appliances, ed. J.E. McMahon and I. Turiel.

Energy Efficiency in Household Appliances, 10-12 November 1997, Florence, Italy, ed. Bertoldi, Ricci and Huenges Wajer, (Springer, Berlin) 1999.

IEA, Proceedings of the *International Energy Conference on Use of Efficiency Standards in Energy Policy,* Sophia-Antipolis, France, 4-5 June 1992, OECD, Paris.

IEA Heat Hump Centre, Heat Pump Energy Efficiency Regulations and Standards, Analysis Report no. HPC-AR4, (Sittard, The Netherlands) June 1996.

International Institute for Energy Conservation (IIEC), Proceedings Summary of the *Forum on Asia Regional Cooperation on Energy Efficiency Standards and Labeling,* Bagkok, Thailand, 14-16 July 1997.

McMahon, J.E., M.A. Piette, and J. Kollar, Lawrence Berkeley National Laboratory, *Office Equipment: Market Characteristics, Energy Use, and Standards Harmonisation,* prepared for the IEA with support from the Japanese New Energy and Industrial Technology Development Organisation (NEDO), April 1995.

Weil, S. and J. McMahon, Lawrence Berkeley National Laboratory, *Energy Efficiency Labels and Standards: A Guidebook for Appliances, Equipment and Lighting,* forthcoming.

United Nations Economic and Social Commission for Asia and the Pacific (ESCAP), United Nations Development Programme (UNDP) and the International Institute for Energy Conservation (IIEC), Proceedings of the *Regional Workshop on Energy Efficiency Standards and Labeling,* Singapore, September 1994.

Order Form

OECD BONN CENTRE

c/o DVG mbh (OECD)
Birkenmaarstrasse 8
D-53340 Meckenheim, Germany
Tel: (+49-2225) 926 166
Fax: (+49-2225) 926 169
E-mail: oecd@dvg.dsb.net
Internet: www.oecd.org/bonn

OECD MEXICO CENTRE

Edificio INFOTEC
Av. San Fernando No. 37
Col. Toriello Guerra
Tlalpan C.P. 14050, Mexico D.F.
Tel: (+52-5) 528 10 38
Fax: (-52-5) 606 13 07
E-mail: mexico.contact@oecd.org
Internet: rtn.net.mx/ocde

OECD CENTRES

*Please send your order
by mail, fax, or by e-mail
to your nearest
OECD Centre*

OECD TOKYO CENTRE

Landic Akasaka Building
2-3-4 Akasaka, Minato-ku
Tokyo 107-0052, Japan
Tel: (+81-3) 3586 2016
Fax: (+81-3) 3584 7929
E-mail: center@oecdtokyo.org
Internet: www.oecdtokyo.org

OECD WASHINGTON CENTER

2001 L Street NW, Suite 650
Washington, D.C., 20036-4922, US
Tel: (+1-202) 785-6323
Toll-free number for orders:
(+1-800) 456-6323
Fax: (+1-202) 785-0350
E-mail: washington.contact@oecd.org
Internet: www.oecdwash.org

I would like to order the following publications

PUBLICATIONS	ISBN	QTY	PRICE		TOTAL
☐ Energy Labels and Standards	92-64-17691-8		$100.00	FF 700	
☐ Experience Curves for Energy Technology Policy	92-64-17650-0		$80.00	FF 750	
☐ World Energy Outlook: 1999 Insights	92-64-17140-1		$120.00	FF 750	
☐ The Link between Energy and Human Activity	92-64-15690-9		$16.00	FF 100	
☐ Energy Policies of IEA Countries – 1999 Review (Compendium)	92-64-17187-8		$120.00	FF 754	
☐ Electricity Market Reform – An IEA Handbook	92-64-16187-2		$50.00	FF 295	
☐ Nuclear Power: Sustainability, Climate Change and Competition	92-64-16954-7		$60.00	FF 360	
☐ Automotive Fuels for the Future – The Search for Alternatives	92-64-16960-1		$100.00	FF 620	
				TOTAL	

DELIVERY DETAILS

Name   Organisation

Address

Country   Postcode

Telephone   Fax

PAYMENT DETAILS

☐   I enclose a cheque payable to IEA Publications for the sum of $ _____ or FF _____

☐   Please debit my credit card (tick choice).   ☐ Access/Mastercard   ☐ Diners   ☐ VISA   ☐ AMEX

Card no: ⌞_⌐_⌐_⌐_⌐_⌐_⌐_⌐_⌐_⌐_⌐_⌐_⌟

Expiry date: ⌞_⌐_⌐_⌐_⌟   Signature:

IEA PUBLICATIONS, 9, rue de la Fédération, 75739 PARIS Cedex 15
Pre-press by Linéale Production. Printed in France by Sagim
(61 00 06 1 P) ISBN 92-64-17691-8 2000

Cover illustration by Bill Marshall